STO

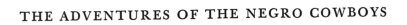

THE ADVENTURES OF THE NEGRO COWBOYS

Also by Philip Durham and Everett L. Jones

THE NEGRO COWBOYS

THE ADVENTURES

of the Negro Cowboys

by Philip Durham and Everett L. Jones

ILLUSTRATED

DODD, MEAD & COMPANY

NEW YORK

Printed in the United States of America
by The Cornwall Press, Inc., Cornwall, N. Y.

Second Printing

The painting by William Henry Jackson is reproduced from the book *The Old West Speaks* by Howard Driggs, illustrated by William Henry Jackson. © 1956 by Prentice-Hall, Inc., Englewood Cliffs, New Jersey.

To
Chris, Pam, and Sam

Preface

The Adventures of the Negro Cowboys is a true history patterned after our longer and more scholarly book called *The Negro Cowboys*. Therefore if one wants to check the sources and references for this work, he should turn to the longer book. There he will find twenty-three pages of notes and fifteen pages of bibliography.

In the "Preface" to the longer book we thanked those many people who helped us in our work. We wish to thank them all again.

PHILIP DURHAM
EVERETT L. JONES

*University of California,
Los Angeles*

Contents

Illustrations

MAPS

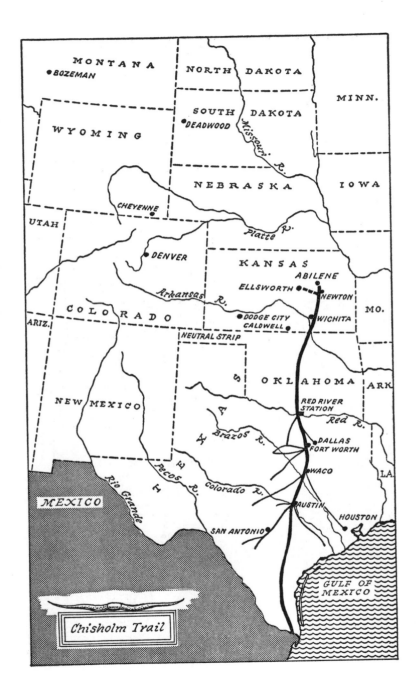

Chisholm Trail

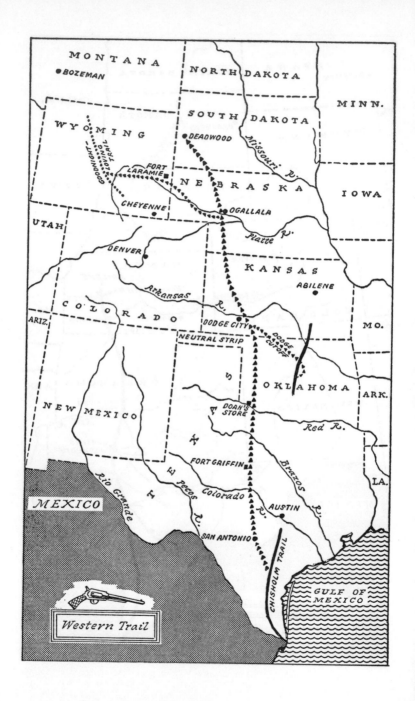

MONTANA
• BOZEMAN

NORTH DAKOTA

MINN.

WYOMING

SOUTH DAKOTA

• DEADWOOD

Missouri R.

GOODNIGHT TRAIL
DAKOTA TRAIL

FORT LARAMIE

NEBRASKA

IOWA

CHEYENNE •

• OGALLALA

UTAH

• DENVER

Platte R.

KANSAS

Arkansas R.

• ABILENE

COLORADO

DODGE CITY •

MO.

ARIZ.

NEUTRAL STRIP

DODGE CITY TRAIL

OKLAHOMA

ARK.

NEW MEXICO

DOAN'S STORE

Red R.

Rio Grande

E. Pecos R.

FORT GRIFFIN

Brazos R.

Colorado R.

AUSTIN

MEXICO

SAN ANTONIO •

CHISHOLM TRAIL

LA.

GULF OF MEXICO

Western Trail

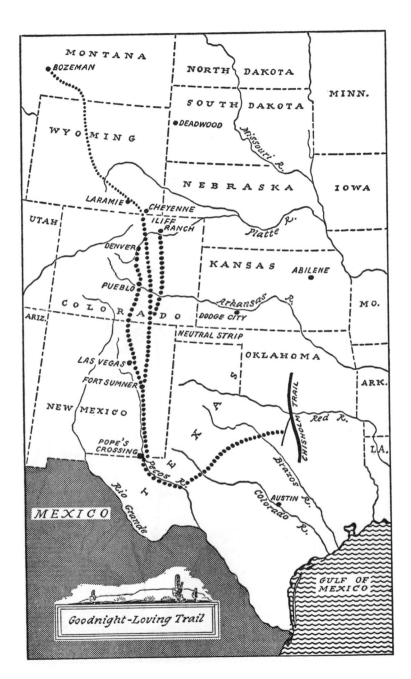

MONTANA

●BOZEMAN

WYOMING

NORTH DAKOTA

SOUTH DAKOTA

●DEADWOOD

MINN.

Missouri R.

NEBRASKA

IOWA

LARAMIE●

UTAH

●CHEYENNE

ILIFF
RANCH

Platte R.

DENVER●

COLORADO

KANSAS

●ABILENE

PUEBLO●

Arkansas R.

MO.

ARIZ.

DODGE CITY●

NEUTRAL STRIP

OKLAHOMA

ARK.

LAS VEGAS●

FORT SUMNER●

NEW MEXICO

POPE'S
CROSSING●

Rio Grande

Pecos R.

Brazos R.

CHISHOLM TRAIL

Red R.

LA.

Colorado R.

AUSTIN●

MEXICO

GULF OF
MEXICO

Goodnight-Loving Trail

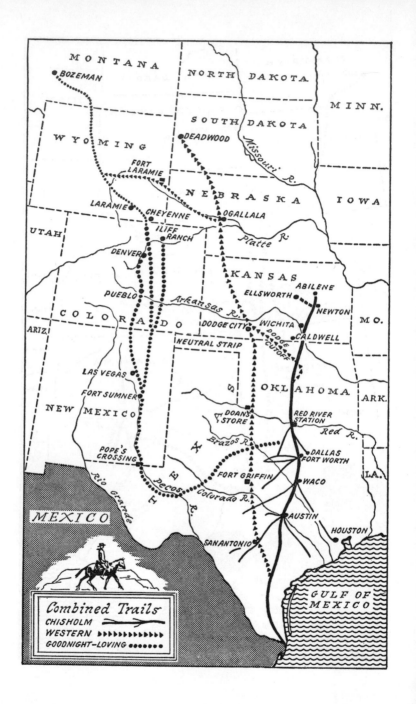

Prologue

✳✳ More than five thousand Negro cowboys rode the trails north from Texas during the years following the Civil War. Some died in stampedes, some froze to death, and some drowned. But most of them lived through long cattle drives to Kansas and the Dakotas or to Colorado and Wyoming.

Some of them were among the best riders on the range. They hunted wild horses and wolves, and a few of them hunted men. Some were villains and some were heroes.

They rode with other Texans, with Mexicans and Indians. All the real cowboys shared the same jobs and dangers. They ate the same food and slept on the same ground.

Years later, when the great plains had been tamed and fenced, the trail drives stopped. Most of the old-time cowboys went back to Texas and took up new kinds of ranching.

But their memories of the old days remained, and they told great tales when they met for reunions or wrote for cattlemen's magazines. Here are the stories they told about the Negro cowboys.

Slaves on Horseback

✳〔ᴅ More than a hundred years ago, before the Civil
War, a crew of bronc-busting cowboys stood outside a large
horse corral. With them was their boss Bradford Grimes, a
cattleman who owned a large South Texas ranch near the
Gulf of Mexico.

Inside the corral was a herd of wild mustangs, horses that
had never been ridden. They milled around, snorting and
rearing.

One of the bronc busters roped a strong stallion and held
him to be saddled. Then another cowboy climbed up and
tried to ride. At first the animal trotted nervously, hump-
ing a little and shying from side to side. Then it went off
in high jumps, spinning and shaking and jolting its rider.
Finally it put its head between its front legs, bucked high
in the air, and threw the cowboy off into the dust.

Just then Mrs. Grimes, the cattleman's wife, came to the
ranch house door and cried out, "Bradford! Bradford!

Those Negroes are worth a thousand dollars apiece. One might get killed."

The cowboys laughed, but they knew she was telling the truth. For they were all Negro slaves. Bradford Grimes was their owner.

Most of the first Negro cowboys were slaves, brought by their masters from the old South. On the plantations in the South, the slaves cut cotton. On the ranches in Texas they had to learn a new trade—breaking horses and handling longhorns. Some were taught by Mexican vaqueros, some by Indians who knew the ways of horses and cattle.

Grimes was only one of hundreds of slave-owning ranchers who ran cattle in Texas. The ranchers had brought their families and slaves from Mississippi, Georgia, and other southern states. They came on horseback, on foot, and in buggies and wagons. They drove hogs, oxen, and stock.

Some ranchers settled near the Mexican border, but there they found that it was too easy for their slaves to escape. Even slaves as far north and east as Austin, the capital of Texas, came to think of Mexico as the promised land. As early as 1845, the year that Texas became a state, a Texas newspaper reported the escape of twenty-five Negroes. "They were mounted on some of the best horses that could be found," the story said, "and several of them were well armed." Thousands of other Negro slaves escaped in the same way.

East of the Nueces River, farther from the Mexican border, most slaves found it hard to escape. So there they stayed, learning to become cowboys in bleak, rough country and learning to chase wild cattle through heavy coastal brush.

All-Negro cattle crews were common throughout central and eastern Texas. There were even a few free Negroes who owned ranches before the Civil War. Aaron Ashworth was one of them, and he owned 2,500 cattle, as well as some slaves of his own. He employed a white schoolmaster to tutor his children.

During the slave days, Negro cowboys learned more than the cattle business. They also learned to fight Indians. Those who were careless or unlucky were killed by Comanche raiders or carried off as captives. Those who learned to fight or run usually lived to carry on the work of ranch and range. They worked with their white masters and with Mexican vaqueros. And slowly they helped to tame and settle a wild country.

CHAPTER 2

Free Men and Wild Cattle

✳️⧽ After the Civil War, the Negro cowboys were free men. Yet they continued to work at the only trade they knew. They signed on with their old masters or with other ranchers and went on working with cattle.

Now that they were free men they took the same risks as all other cowboys. They were no longer valuable property themselves. They not only had the routine work of ranch and range, but they were hired to ride bucking outlaw horses. They sat in dangerous saddles, taking the shocks of bucking, sometimes bleeding from nose and mouth, sometimes fainting, risking rupture, mutilation, or death.

They suffered from some discrimination, but they were luckier than most ex-slaves. They had learned their trade well, and good men were scarce. In cattle outfits they were organized like army squads, with Negroes and whites usually working together. In such an organization, Negro cowboys were welcomed, though only a few became foremen or trail bosses. Jim Perry, who worked for more than twenty years as a great rider, roper, and trail cook, once said, "If it weren't for my damned old black face, I'd have been a boss long ago." One of the white cowboys who rode with him agreed, saying that he no doubt would have been.

During the first years after the end of the Civil War, Negro cowboys helped to round up and brand millions of Texas cattle that had run wild for a long time. The animals were scattered on the plains. They lurked in the brush and hid in the draws and canyons. During more than four years of war, hundreds of thousands of calves had grown to wild cows and longhorned bulls. They were unbranded, unclaimed, untamed, and dangerous.

Out onto the plains and into the brush rode the cowboys. One such man was Henry Beckwith, a Negro who hunted cattle in thickets so dense that neither horse, man, nor cattle could see for more than a few yards. He and his horse found their way by sniffing the air and listening for the sounds of heavy animals crashing through the brush.

Beckwith spent long hours working alone, finding and branding wild cattle. He carried a gun, a length of good rope, and a number of shorter pieces for hog-tying animals. Much of the time he rode at night, stalking in darkness. Therefore the other cowboys called him "the Coyote."

When he needed to sleep, he threw down an old horse-blanket and lay on it. Sometimes he slept in a dried cattle-run or on a pile of dried sticks. Like a coyote, he needed little sleep. If it was cold he built a very small fire and hunched down over it, drinking coffee and dozing. Or he just "wallowed a couple of times" and then got back on his horse.

Like many other cowboys, he carried a bag full of cornbread and dried beef. He drank his coffee strong, and he mixed it with chili juice. Because he spent so much time alone, he rarely talked. He was almost as silent as the animals he hunted.

But he knew his business, and he and thousands of other cowboys located and branded the wild cows and bulls of Texas. Then their bosses looked for some place to sell beef.

There was no market in Texas. According to one old cowhand, "It soon got to the point where a Texas stockman's poverty was reckoned by the number of cattle he owned. The more he had, the poorer he was." Cattle were so cheap that they were hardly worth stealing.

Some cattlemen set up big factories on the Brazos River. They drove herds of longhorn cattle there, and Negro hands butchered the animals, ripped off the hides for leather, and melted down the fat for soap and candle making. Then they threw the meat into the river. Catfish ate the meat and grew to enormous size. Near the mouth of the river on the Gulf of Mexico, the meat attracted so many sharks that people did not dare to swim.

But only the catfish and the sharks could make much profit from such a wholesale slaughter and waste of good cattle. Texas needed markets. Everyone knew that the people in the great cities of the East were hungry for beef. So were those in mining camps and on Indian reservations. Any of these places could be a profitable market for a cattleman who could push a herd of cattle long miles through deserts or flooded rivers, around poisoned water holes and raiding Indians.

Some cattlemen were willing to try. So they rounded up

thousands of cattle and picked out those best able to travel. They organized trail crews and waited for spring. Then they began long trail drives, pushing herds of cattle toward market.

CHAPTER 3

On the Trail

✳️   Texas cattlemen quickly learned how to organize and manage their trail crews.

They learned that the number of cattle in a trail herd should not be much over twenty-five hundred. If they tried to drive many more, the herd became a slow and dangerous monster. An enormous herd was hard to keep moving on a trail or keep together at night. Its size made it unusually dangerous if it hit a flooded river or was startled into a stampede.

Some big herds did go up the trail anyway, but they proved hard to handle. One cowboy told what happened when he was helping to drive a herd of four thousand cattle. One night it stampeded, and he tried to turn the lead steers away from a ditch.

It was a dark night. The cattle were running blindly, packed close together. He rode hard toward the front of the herd, trying to overtake the leaders.

He knew that a ravine lay just ahead. If he could not

turn the cattle, they would pour blindly over a small cliff and pile up at the bottom. Hundreds could be killed.

Finally he pulled alongside the front of the herd. But then he was helpless. Nothing he did could make the leaders turn. Finally they reached the ravine, and the herd roared over the edge. So did the cowboy and his horse, though they were not hurt.

Later he learned what had happened.

"I was trying to point the herd away from the ditch, and a Negro cowboy, Russ Jones, was on the opposite side of the herd trying to do the same thing. The result was that instead of pointing them away from the ditch, we drove them straight into it."

The mistake was expensive. In this one stampede the cowboys lost more than four hundred head of cattle—a loss of thousands of dollars. And the whole catastrophe might have been prevented if the herd had been smaller.

Therefore exceptionally large herds rarely went up the trails. Herds smaller than twenty-five hundred were sometimes seen, but they were expensive to drive. Whenever possible, they were thrown together to make a more efficient operation. Any herd, no matter how small, required at least a minimum crew for a long drive. An average crew contained about eleven men—a trail boss, eight cowboys, a horse wrangler, and a cook.

On a drive, the trail boss was like the captain of a ship. He had absolute authority, and he demanded and received complete cooperation and loyalty. He made all important decisions, anticipating hazards, controlling the speed of the herd, choosing the stopping places each night, and figuring the distances between watering holes. Frequently he owned the herd, but sometimes he was a ranch foreman or a professional trail driver.

During each day, the cowboys worked as a team. Usually two rode "on point," riding near the lead cattle to head them in the right direction and to slow or halt them when necessary. Four more rode "on swing," two patrolling on each side of the herd to keep it strung out and to keep cattle from straying too far off the trail. And the last two, riding "on drag," stayed with the stragglers at the rear and ate the dust of the herd.

The cowboys waited all winter for the day in the spring when they started up the trail, driving a herd of longhorns. It was exciting. Everything was on the move. There were dangers ahead, but the dangers only made life more thrilling.

The two riding on point were usually the more experienced cowboys. They earned the right to lead the others. The four riding swing had more ground to cover. They had to ride up and down the long column, making sure that a longhorn did not stray away. If it did, it had to be driven back. Sometimes an unruly steer could give a cowboy a lot of trouble.

Riding drag was thought to be the worst job. The newest and youngest cowboys had to begin at the end of the line. Not only did they ride all day in the dust from the herd, but the cowboys on drag had to work very hard to make the slow steers keep up with the others.

How the cowboys operated depended in part on the cattle they drove. A beef herd, all steers, traveled fairly fast, sometimes as much as fifteen miles in a day, although no trail boss wanted to push his cattle so hard that they lost weight on the trail. A "wet herd," made up entirely of cows, traveled more slowly. It started early in the spring and grazed up the trail, with calves being born almost every day. On short drives, one cowboy drove a calf wagon to carry the newborn calves and let them out at night to join their mothers.

With mixed herds that traveled faster, it was sometimes impossible to save the calves. Ed Nichols described how Ab Blocker, one of the most famous of the trail bosses, handled the problem. "A big six-foot Negro named Frank was known as Blocker's roper. He didn't work with the herd at night like the rest of the boys; he just did the roping. When they rounded up the cattle to start on the trail there were generally a number of young calves. These were too young to travel and, if there was no one to give them to, Frank shot them and with the help of the other men drove the mothers off. When night came it was his job to rope and hobble these cows to keep them from going back. He had four good roping horses and was the best hand with a rope I ever saw."

As a roping specialist, Frank was excused from night herding. All the other cowboys rode night watch, usually riding two at a time. Sometimes, if the night was calm and the cattle were quiet, only one cowboy would take each shift. He knew how to tell time by the stars and would wake another cowboy when his shift was finished.

One Negro cowboy was a tenderfoot, and so his first night shift never ended. The other cowboys put him on the first night guard and told him to call his relief when the North Star set.

He did as he was told. He rode around the herd, singing softly and looking at the North Star every once in a while. But it never moved. He kept riding and singing, and all the other stars moved around the heavens. Only the North Star remained motionless.

The next morning he rode into camp, tired and sleepy-eyed. The other cowboys were enjoying their coffee after a good night's sleep. They also enjoyed laughing at their practical joke. The tenderfoot's first lesson in astronomy had been a hard one.

A trail drive to Kansas or Wyoming could take two or three long months. A cowboy had to be willing to work day and night under all kinds of conditions. In an eleven-man crew that took twenty-four-hour responsibility for twenty-five hundred longhorn cattle, there was no place for a loafer. Everyone had to do his share, and no one could let down. In a crisis, every cowboy stayed in the saddle indefinitely.

One Negro cowboy named George died in his saddle. He was working on the cold windswept plains of the Texas Panhandle. He didn't have enough clothing because he was a bad gambler and he always lost most of his money playing cards. But he was a good cowboy.

"We all had colds and coughs," one of his friends said. "It was like a bunch of Texas pot hounds baying a 'possum when we tried to sleep. One bitter night I was near George on herd and tried to get him to go to the chuck wagon and turn his horse loose, but he was too game for that. His teeth were chattering as he said to me, 'I can stand it if the rest of you all can.' Presently I saw him lean over his saddle horn, coughing, and he looked like he was losing his breath. By the time I got to him he was off his horse, as dead as a mackerel and as stiff as a poker."

Modern doctors might have known why he died, but the other cowboys said that George had frozen to death. They wrapped his body in his blankets and put it in the chuck wagon. Then they drove to the highest hill they could find in the Palo Duro country. There they dug a grave in the sandy soil, deep enough so that coyotes could not claw into it, and there they buried him.

Few cowboys froze to death, but all of them rode long hours through wind and rain. Some drowned in river crossings when the water ran high, and others were killed by stampeding herds. Some fell in fights with Indians, outlaws, or hostile settlers. But most of them survived all the dangers of their work and even complained of boredom. They learned to bear the tiresome routine of drive and night herd, of saddle and hard ground, of plain food and little sleep. Only after a thousand miles of blistering sun, choking dust, and drenching rain did the cowboys arrive at the end of the trail.

During the trip the members of the crew—the boss, the cowboys, the cook, and the wrangler—built up a close relationship that was little disturbed by differences of race or color. There was some discrimination, of course, but the job was too hard to allow for much nonsense. A cowboy's ability to do his work, to handle his share and a little extra, was far more important than his color. To be a good cowboy, one needed first of all to be a good man, for a mad longhorn would just as soon charge a white Texan as a Negro.

Many of the men who wrote of their days on the plains did not describe the color or nationality of the cowboys with whom they rode. One finds books in which a cowboy is remembered by name, and then pages later is identified, almost by chance, as a Negro. Yet George W. Saunders, once the president of the Old Time Trail Drivers Association, estimated that about a third of the 35,000 cowboys who drove up the trails from Texas were Negroes or Mexicans.

A typical crew had two or three Negroes among its eight cowboys. Its boss was usually white, although a few Negroes ran their own outfits. The wrangler could be either Negro or Mexican. The cook was likely to be a Negro—usually an ex-cowboy.

The horse wrangler on a drive had the hardest work to do. Sometimes he had to take care of as many as sixty horses because every cowboy needed more than one horse. The horses became tired. When a horse tired, its rider rode in and got a fresh one.

The wrangler rose early each morning, called by the last night herder or the cook. He took his own horse, which he had picketed nearby, and rode off to bring in the other horses so that the cowboys could choose their first mounts of the day. Then he gathered the spares, ordinarily going ahead of the cattle, staying near the chuck wagon. At night he chose new grazing grounds for his horses. He picked spots well away from the herd, yet close enough to the camp that he could watch them. If he hobbled the horses, they rarely strayed very far.

But sometimes they disappeared. One Negro wrangler, working in rugged country near the Pecos River, woke to find all his horses gone. Seven hours later he found two of them twelve miles away. Not until several days later did he catch them all.

On some trails a wrangler had to guard against many dangers. The horses themselves were frequently mean and only half broken. Sometimes a drive went through Indian country where Indians might steal the horses. And in raw, unsettled country, there might be wolves with a taste for horseflesh.

Rattlesnakes could always spook the horses. Or even worse, they could bite the wrangler, who spent more time afoot than any other member of the crew except possibly the cook. Once bitten, he could expect rough treatment. On one cattle drive, for instance, a Negro wrangler named Dick came back to the camp sucking his thumb where a rattlesnake had struck him. His hand and arm were already badly swollen.

Seeing what had happened, one of the other cowboys immediately drew a knife and gashed the thumb around the fang marks. Then he opened a pistol cartridge, poured powder over the wound, and lighted it with a match. Dick seems to have survived both the bite and the treatment.

Even more surprisingly, he and most other wranglers managed to live through all the work they had to do. The wrangler rose before dawn, tended and drove horses all day. He was never off duty for more than a moment until the last night herder had roped his horse and the other horses had been hobbled. And he was also expected to drag up wood for the fire, help the cook load and unload the chuck wagon, and even wash dishes. He had good reason to want to be a regular cowboy, if only to escape the cook, who could be a tyrant.

The cook was so important, in fact, that he deserves a separate chapter.

CHAPTER 4

Cooks and Their
Chuck Wagons

✻✻ When Charlie Siringo, one of the first cowboy writers, described his life as a young man in southern Texas, he remembered the food he ate in roundup camps and on cattle drives.

"Meals were made up of meat from a fat heifer calf, with corn bread, molasses, and black coffee," he said. "The Negro cook generally had two kinds of meat, the calf ribs broiled before the camp-fire, and a large Dutch oven full of loin, sweet-breads, and heart, mixed with flour gravy."

There were hundreds of Negro cooks who drove chuck wagons on roundups and cattle drives. Some cooked meals that men remembered fondly for decades: sourdough biscuits that floated, beef swimming in brown gravy, beans bubbling in large kettles, and bread pudding, sweetened with raisins and molasses. Other cooks were remembered because they cooked badly. Their steaks were tough, their coffee weak, and their biscuits like rocks. But good or bad, the cooks were never forgotten.

A trail cook could be any race or nationality. He might be a white Texan, a Negro, a Mexican, or even a "Portugee." He was sometimes called "the old woman," but all cowboys agreed that he very rarely acted like a lady. More often than not, he was one of the toughest men in the crew. As one writer said, the cook was sometimes "hard-featured and unlovely, with a bad temper and perhaps a few notches on his gun." Certainly most cowboys thought that "crossing a cook is as risky as braiding a mule's tail."

Often the cook was merely cranky rather than mean. He had many duties, and he had to keep some kind of order in camp. He had to produce meals at all times, whether the day was calm or the wind blew. Normally he stopped with his wagon headed into the wind and then built his fire behind it. One old cowboy remembered that "anyone riding up to the wagon was supposed to approach behind the fire so that no sand would blow into the skillets and ovens. Any green puncher who, not knowing this law, violated it, was likely to learn it soon enough, by being told the names of his ancestors and kinfolk."

Whether cranky or cheerful, Negro or white, the "old woman" was recognized as an important member of the crew. Any cowboy who failed to show respect soon learned that he had made a mistake. The cowboy could find his coffee bitter and full of grounds. His beans were cold and hard, or burned and black. His meat was full of gristle. His blankets were frequently misplaced, and his comfort was disturbed by countless accidents. The cook could take a terrible revenge.

He was usually one of the oldest men in the outfit, frequently a cowboy who could no longer take the punishment of twelve to sixteen hours a day in the saddle. He was responsible not only for the crew's food, but also for their bedrolls and personal possessions, which rode in his wagon. Often he acted as doctor, dentist, or older brother, and it was he who dosed the cowboys when they were ill, listened to them when they were depressed, and amused them when they were bored.

His wagon was their home. Each morning it pulled out ahead of the herd, carrying the food, the bedrolls, and even the boss's papers. Each night it stopped at a new place, where the cook built a fire and set out a fresh pot of coffee.

The chuck wagon was a sturdy vehicle, usually one with iron axles and wide tires. It had a flat bed, under which was fastened a barrel large enough to carry a water supply for two days. A chuck box for holding food and cooking utensils was built onto the back of the wagon. Fastened to the box was a leaf which could be let down to form a work table for the cook. In the wagon itself, which ordinarily was covered by a canvas sheet, were flour, beans, sugar, coffee, bacon, salt pork, molasses, canned tomatoes—the staples of the trail diet. There, too, were the personal possessions of the crew, as well as rude medicines, a few tools, and perhaps a little grain for the harness stock.

The cook had to be an expert mule skinner or bullwhacker as well as an artist with a heavy frying pan. Driving the chuck wagon over rough country, he led the way up the trail each day to the new stopping place the boss had chosen. Then he made a new home for the crew. A good cook who could do these things, no matter how hard-bitten he might be, was indispensable.

John Young, an old cowboy, remembered such a man. "The one man in our outfit that I recall most often and most vividly was Sam, the Negro cook," Young said. "He always had a cheerful word or a cheerful song, and he seemed to have an affection for every one of us. When we camped in the vicinity of brush every cowboy before coming in would rope a chunk of wood and snake it up to the chuck wagon. That wood always made Sam grinning happy whether he needed it or not."

Sam was also an entertainer. He carried along a banjo, which he played until one of the boys accidentally stepped on it. Then the crew chipped in and bought him a fiddle, which he also played, picking or sawing out airs like "Green Corn, Green Corn."

Sam was thirty-five years old and he weighed 225 pounds, so he was a bit too old and too heavy for the active life of a cowboy. But he was still a good rider, and frequently one of the crew got him to ride and gentle an unruly horse. Once in the saddle, he stuck like a burr, and the horse soon tired of trying to throw his heavy load.

One day in camp another cowboy looked at Sam's great bulk and shook his head.

"You're too big and strong to be just a man," he said. "But you're not big enough to be a horse."

Sam laughed. "I *am* a horse," he said, "and I'll bet a dollar no man in the outfit can ride me without spurs."

That started a new game. When the crew camped for the night in a sandy place, Sam stripped down to his long underwear and tied a bandanna around his neck for a bridle.

One after another the cowboys took off their boots and mounted his back. And one after another they were thrown down into the soft sand by the human "horse" who could anticipate and bewilder the reactions of his riders. None of them earned a dollar that night.

Whenever the boys stayed in one place long enough to do a bit of hunting, Sam did a lot of cooking. If he had time to barbecue antelope ribs or to roast buffalo steaks or a wild turkey, the crew expected what Sam called a "wedding feast"—a wedding of dinner and supper. They stood around the campfire looking hungry and waiting for his call. Then it came.

"Wash your face, comb your hair, and come and get it while she's hot and juicy," he always shouted. And the crew came fast.

Sam had no reason to fear horses or men. But he was badly frightened for a moment on one calm sunny afternoon. The cattle were grazing quietly on the Texas plain while the crew loafed near the chuck wagon. Suddenly all the boys were startled by Sam's cry, a wild yell so unusual that some of them sprang to their horses and drew their guns.

Sam was pointing at the sky. They looked up and saw the beginning of an eclipse, a blot on the sun that grew until the day was dark and the stars came out. No available newspaper had predicted it, and Sam—like many other frontier folk that day—feared that the end of the world was coming. But enough of the boys knew about eclipses to explain what was happening.

Sam's abilities as a cook, a rider, and a musician became known far and wide. His outfit was envied by other cowboys on the trail, for some of them traveled with cooks who burned their meat, watered their coffee, and grumbled day and night.

One Negro cook named Zeno was long remembered by the crew for whom he cooked. Ordinarily he did well enough, but once he made a bad mistake.

He always kept his baking soda in a wide-mouthed pickle jar. And he kept a supply of calomel—a powerful laxative—in another pickle jar. Almost inevitably the day came when he confused the two and baked up a batch of bread full of calomel.

The bread tasted a little strange, but the men ate it for supper and then sat around the campfire for a few hours before bedding down. Soon they began disappearing, and few of them did any sleeping. "We were a sick lot," one said. Zeno was very unpopular for a long time.

Usually cooks carried guns, for a chuck wagon driven in front of the herd was a lonely and dangerous position. Some cooks developed a healthy fear of Indians and a boastful pride in their own superior skill as gunmen. A Negro cooking for an 1868 trail crew demonstrated both at once.

When one of the cowboys found a five-dollar bill on the trail, the cook challenged him to a contest. This is how the cowboy told the story:

"One day at dinner the Negro cook offered to bet me a two-year-old heifer he had in the herd against my five dollars that he could beat me shooting, only one shot each. I was good with a pistol, but I knew the cook was hard to beat. But I did not get nervous, as the two-year-old was about six to one if I won. One of the boys got a little piece of a board, took a coal out of the campfire, made a black spot about the size of a twenty-five-cent piece, stepped off fifteen steps (about forty-five feet) and yelled, 'All ready, shoot.'

"I was to shoot first. I jerked my old cap-and-ball Navy pistol out, and just about one second before I pulled the trigger I saw the heads of six Indians just over a little rise in the ground, coming toward camp. This excited me so that I did not hit the spot—only about one-half of my bullet touched the board just to the right of the target.

"I yelled to the cook, 'Shoot quick! Look at the Indians!' By that time we could see them plainly on top of the rise. He fired, but never touched the board. So six big Osage Indians saved me my valuable find—the five-dollar bill."

The six big Indians proved to be friendly, and their arrival was painful only to the cook.

At other times and on other drives, Indians were hostile. Sometimes they attacked the herd, attempting to kill or drive off beef for their tribes. Sometimes they tried to steal the wrangler's horses. And occasionally they surrounded the camp, threatening the crew and trying to blackmail the boss for tobacco, guns, and cattle.

One crew driving a herd to Nebraska found themselves surrounded by thirty heavily armed and menacing Indians. They were outnumbered nearly three to one, and the situation looked hopeless.

Then the Negro cook got an idea. He began to lurch around the chuck wagon and pretend that he was insane. He put on quite a show.

The Indians immediately got on their horses and rode away. One of the cowboys in the crew told the story later and explained, "An Indian won't stay where there is a crazy person. They say he is the devil."

But Indians were rare interruptions on most long cattle drives. Usually the two or three months on the trail were more monotonous than exciting. By the time the crew reached their destination and delivered their cattle, all of the men were so bored that any of them could act a little crazy.

Consequently Gordon Davis, a Negro cook for Ab Blocker's crew, arrived in Dodge City and paraded down the main street riding on his left wheel ox, fiddle in hand, playing "Buffalo Girls, Can't You Come Out Tonight." Another Negro cook celebrated the end of a drive by becoming the first prisoner of Abilene's jail.

Soon after the Civil War, Abilene, Kansas, became the first of the roaring cowtowns. Because it was a market place and railroad-shipping point for cattle, it was a busy city every summer. Thousands of cattle came up the trail to fill its pens and graze on the surrounding plains. Cowboys rode into town and washed off sweat and dirt with tubs of hot water. They filled the barber shops and came out clipped and shaved and smelling of bay rum. They roamed from saloon to saloon, played cards with the gamblers, and got into fights.

The town quickly built a new jail to hold troublemakers. And the Negro cook became its first prisoner. He rode into town and bought a meal that someone else had cooked. After that, he drowned his memories of smoky campfires with too many glasses of Abilene whiskey. Then he began shooting up the town—not doing much damage, but making a lot of noise.

The town marshal came running and managed to disarm the drunken cook, arrest him, and throw him into jail.

The cook stayed in jail until his hungry trail crew learned where he was. They mounted their horses and rode into town. They drove the marshal into hiding, shot the lock off the door, and freed the cook. Then they galloped past the office of the town trustees and shot it full of holes. Finally, having rescued their man and expressed their contempt for the town's government, they rode back to camp.

Thus a Negro cook posted two records: he was the first man thrown into the new jail, and the first man to break out.

Stampedes and River Crossings

❄ξd Every cattle drive started with some confusion. Even after the cattle had been rounded up and thrown together in a trail herd, they remained wild, irritable, and unpredictable. At the beginning they lacked unity or leadership, and every steer was a possible troublemaker.

During the first week the trail boss pushed the herd as hard as he could. He might even risk running a little weight off prime animals and losing a few head of the weaker stock. He wanted to be sure that the longhorns became tired enough to be quiet. During that week he and his crew learned the peculiarities of the herd and identified its leaders and its troublesome animals. Soon it stretched out on the trail each day and moved steadily forward.

Each night the drive ended at a so-called "bed ground," preferably an area that offered some water and fresh grass for the cattle. They had nipped at grass all day on the trail, but now they began steady grazing. Then slowly they settled down one by one for a fitful night's sleep. The cowboys on night herd, working in shifts, rode slowly around them.

Usually the cowboy sang, not to entertain themselves or the cattle, but to keep the longhorns from taking fright. Because a cowboy who rode silently could startle a herd in the night, every night herder sang or chanted constantly.

One Negro cowboy was known as Big Mouth Henry because "he was a great singer and could almost charm a bunch of Longhorns."

But not even endless singing could always reassure a restless herd. If the weather changed suddenly and a thunderstorm rolled in, a flash of lightning could set the herd off in a wild stampede.

Sometimes the violent storms of the high plains frightened even the cowboys. Many of them were killed by lightning, and all of them learned to fear the nights when balls of fire seemed to play around the horns of the cattle, when even the grass was set aflame and the air smelled like sulphur. Sitting tall in their saddles, cowboys were like living lightning rods.

Their cattle could go on a blind and headless stampede, taking out over the plain in a wild run, scattering in all directions. If a beast faltered or fell, it was trampled and killed by the rest of the herd. If the lead steers plunged over the edge of a gully, much of the herd followed, piling bodies on bodies.

Therefore cowboys always remembered the big stampedes. One wrote of a black night on the Old Chisholm Trail. "Just after nightfall," he said, "we had a severe storm with lots of thunder, lightning, and cold. It was so dark most of the hands left us and went to the chuck wagon except W. T. Henson, myself, and old Chief, a Negro." Then the herd took fright and ran, fanning out across the land, running out of control. The three night herders could not turn or control it. It broke up and scattered so widely that it took the whole crew more than two days to get it back together.

It did not take lightning or thunder to start a stampede. Any unusual sight or sound could do it. Herds were set off by the sudden snort of a restless steer; they jumped and ran if the cook dropped a tin pan.

One cowboy described his first stampede. "Early in the night," he said, "it had rained, and I was on the watch. The herd began drifting, and the boss and several others came out to help with the cattle. After the rain ceased we got them stopped. Then Rany Fentress, a Negro who had been in stampedes before, came to where I was in the lead and told me to move farther away. About that time one of the boys struck a match to light a pipe, and the flare frightened the big steers and they began to run. I was knocked down three times, but managed to stay with the pony. I came out with the drag riders and stayed with them until daylight."

Another stampede was started by a deer. "One night a severe thunderstorm came up," an old cowboy wrote. "The horses had been turned loose when, just before the storm started, a deer jumped up in front of the herd and caused them to stampede. They ran directly by camp, causing the horses to join them and came near leaving the cowboys all afoot.

"The wrangler's horse was the only one staked. As one of the boys ran to mount him, he got frightened, pulled up his stake and went rushing by camp. The Negro cook, taking in the situation, grabbed the rope and went bumping along for about a hundred yards before he could stop him. He then mounted and assisted in trying to stop the herd."

Ordinarily a stampeding herd could be turned or stopped before it had run more than a mile. But some herds took off so fast and ran so hard that they ended up scattered over an area of twenty miles or more. On one dark night in the Indian Territory, now Oklahoma, a herd took off and scattered widely. In that stampede Joe Tasby, a Negro cowboy, got separated from the rest of the crew and rode for more than twenty-four hours before he found his way back to what remained of the herd.

A stampede was only one of the dangers a cowboy faced on a long trail drive. As one trail driver said, "Everything was then tough, wild and woolly, and it was dangerous to be safe." Some of the toughest parts of every drive were the long drives to water and the sometimes dangerous river crossings.

One drive included a long, dry run in Texas from Oasis Springs to the Red River. It was made by James Cowan, his wife, and three children, aided by a Negro cook whose nickname was Snowball. To help drive the cattle, Cowan hired some Texas cowboys.

Cowan's wife drove one wagon loaded with the children and household goods. Snowball drove the chuck wagon, and Cowan himself drove a third wagon behind the herd to try to save some of the newborn calves. All three wagons were drawn by oxen.

The last part of the drive to the Red River was a nightmare. "A nightmare," Cowan's son said later, "that I can never erase from memory—the bawling of cattle, the groaning of men and horses, and the rattle of chains in the ox-yoke rings." As the herd came close to the river, both the oxen and the cattle smelled water and started to run. Cowan's wife stopped her wagon by shooting the near ox of her team, and the cowboys stopped Snowball's chuck wagon by roping his oxen.

The herd stampeded—catching, trampling, and killing one cowboy. Then it ran until it was widely scattered up and down the bank of the Red River. It took days for Cowan to round up all his cattle. But fortunately the river was low and he was able to cross without further difficulty.

Other cattlemen were less lucky, and they came to rivers that were flooding. Then the fast, rough water was a potential killer, and dangerous river crossings took men's lives.

Many cowboys could not swim at all, and few were strong swimmers. The tricky currents of high, muddy rivers were made even more dangerous by floating tree trunks and branches and by hidden rocks and snags. Through these dangers the cowboys tried to drive their struggling cattle and horses.

If the cowboys were lucky, the steers swam straight across without accident. One cowboy said, "It was a wonderful sight to see a thousand steers swimming all at one time. All you could see was the tips of their horns and the ends of their noses as they went through the water." The wagons were floated across, with men riding by the oxen to guide them.

But if a river was really flooding, a cattle crossing could be a terrible experience. Whenever it rained in the Wichita Mountains, for instance, the Red River became an angry monster. Then it looked a mile wide. Its rapid current boiled up in great brown waves and cut large holes in its banks. It carried such a mass of broken trees and tangled branches that it looked as if it had uprooted a forest.

It stopped many drives in their tracks. Once cattlemen were holding more than 60,000 steers on the south rim of the Red River, waiting for the waters to fall. With all those cattle held close together, the danger of a disastrous stampede worried everybody.

Sure enough, after two anxious days and nights, a herd took fright and began to run. Soon all the cattle were milling around in the darkness. Steers were knocked down and trampled to death. All the trail drivers suffered losses, and their crews spent ten days sorting out their cattle.

Risks like these made cowboys take even more dangerous chances in trying to cross flooding rivers. Many of them were knocked down by floating tree trunks or frantic cattle. Some were drowned.

Not all cowboys were so lucky as the Negro who had a narrow escape when he tried to cross the flooding Canadian River. Near the middle, his horse sank under him and left him stranded on a sandbar. Another cowboy rode to his rescue. Swimming his horse to the sandbar, the cowboy told the Negro to hang on to the horse's tail and then swam the horse back, pulling the man behind him. Once ashore, the rescued cowboy was more than grateful.

"That horse's tail," he said, "was just like the hand of Providence."

Another Negro cowboy was saved by a steer. Tony Williams was one of a trail crew trying to cross the swollen Red River in 1873. He got aboard a mule and rode point to lead the herd through the dangerous waters. He made it well out into the river, with all the cattle strung out behind him.

Then a big wave caught Tony and knocked him off his mount. He sank out of sight, while his horse and the herd kept struggling to cross.

"We thought he had drowned," one of his friends said. "But in a little while we discovered him holding on to the tail of a big beef steer. When the steer went up the bank Tony was still holding on and went with him."

Tony's adventure was only one episode in a long drive. Every trail driver could tell similar stories. When George Henry Gilland, for instance, made his own drive from Dallas to Dodge City, he fought stampedes, flooded rivers, and other Texans.

He bought a herd of fifteen hundred steers in Dallas. Then he hired a cook and eight cowboys and began the drive north.

During the first few days they rode through settled country, moving the herd over narrow, poorly fenced roads. Then the country opened up somewhat and the steers could graze on the trail.

One night, when Gilland's crew got near the Red River, the weather changed. Big clouds rolled in and blacked out the stars. Thunder made the herd restless. Except for flashes of lightning, Gilland said, "It was a night so dark no object could be seen."

Then the cattle stampeded. The outfit could not turn them or stop them, and they scattered for miles.

The next morning the crew began a roundup. Gilland took Hamm Harris, one of his two Negro cowboys, and trailed one bunch straight down a lane to a closed corral. There he found his steers, but he also found a dozen men lined up on the fence.

"Are these your cattle?" one of them asked.

When Gilland said they were, the farmer claimed that the steers had trampled his cornfield. Backed by his fence-sitting friends, he demanded fifty dollars to release the herd.

Gilland went out to inspect the corn. He found cattle tracks all right, but they were old ones. And he knew that he had followed fresh tracks directly to the corral. So he refused to pay.

Instead, he and Hamm Harris rode straight to the corral. They were both wearing guns, and nobody stopped them. The Negro cowboy opened the gate and guarded it while Gilland drove out the steers.

The farmer and his friends made threats, but nobody reached for a gun. Later Gilland learned from other trail drivers that the farmer made a regular practice of knocking down his own fences and trying to collect damages from cattlemen.

Once he had recovered his cattle, Gilland made a long one-day drive to the Red River. The Red was swift and high, with branches and brush swirling in its muddy current.

The cattle stopped, refusing to enter the water. Finally Gilland lassoed a lead steer and dragged it bawling into the river. Swimming his horse, he half-led, half-pulled the steer across, while the rest of the herd followed.

Now he and his crew were in the Indian Territory of Oklahoma. They drove straight north, using lamed or injured animals to pay the tolls demanded by the Indian tribes. And they crossed the Washita River, the South Canadian, and the Cimarron.

"The Washita," Gilland said, "offered no difficulties, but when we reached the South Canadian we were detained twenty-four hours by a flood which caused it to overflow its banks. When this subsided we crossed without much difficulty. Its north branch was dry and its wide bed of alkali deposits could be seen for miles, glistening white in the sun like snow. The Cimarron River was wide but the cattle had become trail broken and were not afraid to cross, so we reached Dodge City without further incident."

U. S. 1467371

CHAPTER 6

Where the Trails Went

✳❆ The reason for the long cattle drives was that Texas was thousands of miles from the biggest market for beef. In the East, where most Americans lived, there were cattle buyers and meat-packing houses. At about the time of the Civil War the American people began to eat more beef than pork, and there was a great demand for beef.

But there were still no railroads going from Texas to the East. Cattlemen could not ship their animals as they can today. Instead, they had to round them up and drive them to railroads and markets in Kansas, Nebraska, or Colorado.

A look at the map will show that there were three main trails over which cattlemen drove their cattle up from Texas. These were the Chisholm Trail, the Western Trail, and the Goodnight-Loving Trail. They became important as cowboys drove cattle to them from all over the Texas plains.

Once on a main trail, a cattleman drove his herd to a cowtown on a railroad, or to a mining camp or Indian reservation, or to the open grasslands of the north where new ranches were being built. Most of the longhorns were trailed to railheads like Abilene or Ellsworth or Dodge City. To get them there took a lot of careful planning by the trail boss.

To help him, and to get more business from Texas cattlemen, the Kansas Pacific Railway once printed a little book describing the route from the crossing of Red River to Ellsworth, Kansas. This trail, which ran all the way through the Indian Territory of Oklahoma and half way through Kansas, was like most of the trails the cowboys rode in those days.

The Red River Station, as the Chisholm Trail map shows, was on the boundary line between Texas and Oklahoma. By the time a herd reached that point, it was pretty well broken to the trail. Now the cowboys could concentrate on getting their cattle through stormy nights, across such rivers as the North and South Canadian, the Cimarron and the Arkansas, and through the Indian country.

As the herd moved north from the Red River, it went up a small divide which opened out into a prairie. The first night the cowboys bedded the cattle near a branch of Beaver Creek, fifteen miles from the Red. They found an abundance of wood and water. Crossing Beaver Creek was no problem, because at that point the stream was small.

The next day the herd traveled another fifteen miles over high rolling prairie. It stopped that night on Stinking Creek, another small stream easy to ford. Again the cowboys found plenty of wood and water and a good campground.

The third day they trailed across country where timber skirted the trail on both sides. On occasion they passed large groves of oak trees. Thereafter, one day was much like another. If everything went well, an all-steer herd averaged twelve miles a day—even with an occasional layover for a short rest.

On the day before the herd reached the Washita River, it traveled through burned-over jack oak country where there was no water for ten miles. But fording the Washita was not difficult because it had a rock bottom. And that night the cattle had a good bedding ground.

The cowboys stopped the herd on the south side of the Canadian River because they knew there were no good camping grounds on the north side. They also knew that they could cross the river without difficulty the following morning.

The drive continued over the same kind of upland rolling prairie for several days. The cowboys stopped at places like Deer Creek, King Fisher Creek, Red Fork, and Turkey Creek.

If everything went well, the crew reached Turkey Creek on the twelfth day after leaving the Red River. Here they found a good place to rest, not only because there was plenty of wood and water, but also because Turkey Creek had the first supply store the men had seen in twelve days.

For about five of the miles between Turkey Creek and Hackberry Creek, the herd went through "a dog town." A dog town was a large colony or village of prairie dogs, burrowing little rodents that lived throughout the Great Plains from northern Mexico to Montana.

When the cowboys rode through a village of prairie dogs, they frequently took time to stop and grin at the amusing little animals. The prairie dog is about the size of a small cat or puppy. It is either plain gray or reddish buff, with a black tip on its tail. What amused the cowboys was the way in which the prairie dog threw up a mound of dirt at the end of each burrow. Then it sat up and looked around in a cocky manner, trying to give the impression that it had done a great job.

The cowboys rode very carefully through a dog town. Each cowboy and his horse had to watch for prairie dog holes. If the horse stepped into a hole it could fall and break its leg. This meant the loss of a horse and occasionally the loss of a cowboy.

There was no wood at some of the camps in northern Oklahoma: at Hackberry Creek and Nine Mile Creek, for example. So when the outfit stopped at these grounds, it had to bring wood from a previous camp.

Carrying wood along the trail was not easy. The way the cowboys did it was to stretch what they called a "cooney" under the chuck wagon. This was a loose-hanging piece of cowhide, tied to the wagon by each of its four corners. Into this the cowboys could generally pile enough wood so that the cook could get by for an extra few days.

If everything continued well, the outfit reached Pond Creek on the fifteenth day—about 185 miles from the Red River. Here the trail hands found a good camp and a store. It was here, too, that the trail boss had to make a decision about which way he wanted to go.

There was a well-marked old trail, but the trail boss usually decided on the newer route known as Cox's Trail. If he stayed on the old trail, his outfit probably ran into trouble with the many settlers in Sumner, Sedgwick, and Reno counties in Kansas. These counties were now so well populated that the farmers fought against the trail drivers. The farmers knew that the big longhorn herds could damage or destroy their crops.

So when the herd reached Bluff Creek, two days on from Pond Creek, it veered a bit to the west to reach Cox's Crossing. This was the only place for several miles up and down the creek where wagons could cross safely.

Crossing Bluff Creek was not the only problem the cowboys faced at Cox's Crossing. Here they were warned that they would find no wood for several miles, and they were told to take enough for five or six days' use. This much wood so filled the cooney that at times it bumped on the ground.

The cowboys had now traveled clear through Oklahoma and into Kansas, having completed almost two-thirds of their trip from the Texas border to Ellsworth. On about the twentieth day they trailed the herd over high rolling prairie and reached the Ninescah River. Here they could rest for a while. They could also ride a mile and a half east of the crossing to E. C. Manning's store. They could get almost anything they needed at Manning's because he specialized in cattlemen's supplies.

Three days later the trail boss could halt the herd at Indian Run, a small stream able to water large herds. The short buffalo grass all around it made a fine grazing ground.

Or the trail boss could drive on another four miles to Rattlesnake Creek and find an excellent campground, a large supply of water, and grass in abundance.

On the twenty-fourth day out, he could drive the herd across the Arkansas River. The best place—in fact, the only good place—to cross was at Ellinwood, between Great Bend and Raymond. At Ellinwood the country was open and level, and there were no steep bluffs on the river bank. The river was wide, but even at high water it was shallow. Also, there was no quicksand at the Ellinwood crossing.

Assuming that the drive met only the normal hazards of the trail, it arrived at the Kansas Pacific Railroad on the twenty-seventh day—having traveled about 320 miles from the Red River Crossing in Texas.

The railroad had a very large grazing ground around the Kansas towns of Ellsworth, Wilson, Bosland, and Russell. On this high rolling prairie, different trail crews could hold as many as 300,000 cattle at one time while they waited to sell or ship their herds.

Once the cattle had been disposed of, the town of Ellsworth could take care of the cowboys. It was a typical cowtown, complete with barbershop, saloons, gamblers, and gunfire. To a crew of dirty, dusty cowboys it looked like heaven, but a local editor thought it was more like hell. At the very least, it was never dull or quiet.

For a few days a town like Ellsworth or Abilene offered Texas cowboys fun and relaxation. A trail crew shaved and bathed, and drank or gambled. They bought new clothes and mended their saddles and bridles. Some of them even went to Sunday sermons and church suppers. Then almost all of them got on their horses and rode back to Texas.

A few stayed to help settle the northern ranges. And a few died, some from natural causes and some from gunfire.

One who died from natural causes was a cattleman, R. B. Johnson. He took a herd up the old Chisholm Trail to Abilene and then took sick. Soon he was dead. His men had his body embalmed and buried immediately.

Months later one of his Negro cowboys, George Glenn, returned to get the body. He had the casket dug up and loaded into a Studebaker wagon. Then, because there were no railroads between Kansas and Texas, he drove the wagon back to Johnson's old home in Colorado County, Texas.

Glenn made the trip alone, staying on the trail for forty-two days and nights. He recrossed all the rivers and creeks, passing all the old campsites and grazing grounds. Each night he picketed his horses and prepared his own food. Sometimes he started a small cooking fire, but at other times he made a cold meal of beans, bacon, and canned tomatoes. He slept each night in the wagon by the casket.

It was a long, hard trip, but Glenn got the body back to the home ranch for burial in the family cemetery. He demonstrated in his own way the kind of fierce loyalty to boss and outfit that almost every cowboy felt. Years later, when Glenn was an old man, he still was proud of his part in the great trail-driving days. When he got dressed up, he wore on his lapel a copy of his old outfit's trail brand. He wore it like a soldier's decoration.

Not all the Negroes on the Chisholm Trail were cowboys, and not all of them rode horses. At one time many hundreds of them walked up the trail to settle on the Western plains. A famous white cowboy, Charlie Siringo, wrote that he once found the trail lined with Negroes headed for Kansas, where they thought they could get a free farm and a span of mules from the state government. Some of them carried all their possessions on their backs, while others drove donkeys or oxen.

There were many Negro settlements scattered through the Indian Territory (now Oklahoma) and Kansas. There were a few farther north in western Nebraska. The Negroes carved sod huts out of the prairie and dug in to wait out the long cold winter and the wet, windy spring. Then they planted wheat and corn and hay and began to build their farms.

Some got discouraged and went back to the southern states they had come from. Others, like Negro Henry in Nebraska, tried illegal shortcuts. Henry was thrown into a Nebraska jail in 1869 for selling whiskey to the Indians. But more Negroes were like the Shores family, who built a successful farm on the Nebraska frontier and later became well known as musicians. Negro settlers helped to civilize and fence many parts of Oklahoma, Kansas, and Nebraska.

This kind of settlement helped to close the old Chisholm Trail. Soon the pleasant valleys and open rolling plains north of the Red River Crossing were blocked by fences and armed farmers who refused to let large herds of cattle trail through and trample their fields of corn and wheat.

So the cattlemen pioneered a new trail that ran north from Doan's Store on the Red River. It went straight north through the Texas Panhandle to Dodge City in western Kansas. Thousands of cowboys took this new trail and drove millions of cattle to the North. The stories told by old cattlemen and cowboys are full of references to Negro cowboys.

Typical of the most efficient of the Negro cowboys was Jim Kelly. Jim was the son of Arnos and Phoebe Kelly, free Negroes who worked for the Olive family in Texas. Young Jim grew up with the Olive brothers and was a lifelong friend of Print Olive. When Print became the leader of the Olive family, Jim became one of Print's right-hand men.

At one time Jim Kelly was the outfit's horsebreaker. According to Harry E. Chrisman, in his book *The Ladder of Rivers*, "Jim was a peerless horse trainer." The fact that the Olives had some of the finest horses in Texas was credited to Jim, who did the breaking and training. Jim was also the tutor for young Bob Olive in all things pertaining to ranch work: "bronc riding, roping, horse training, and the use of the six-shooter."

In *The Ladder of Rivers* Jim is referred to as "a Negro without fear or shame, who looked all men in the eyes as equals." Furthermore, Print Olive admired Jim Kelly's "disciplined sense of equality and pride of race."

This sense of equality was shared by many men and spread through much of the West as the cattle trails pushed farther North. The Western Trail, for instance, soon extended beyond Dodge City, through Kansas, and into Nebraska. At the town of Ogallala, Nebraska, the trail divided into two main branches, one going westward to Montana and the other going northward to Deadwood City, South Dakota.

Up these northern trails rode many crews of white and Negro cowboys who worked and played together without prejudice or friction. When a French nobleman, Baron de Mandat-Grancey, visited the Black Hills of Dakota one year, he saw a group of cowboys amusing themselves on the street in front of a saloon. They were practicing roping and doing some wrestling. The Baron, who had heard much about race prejudice in America, was astonished to see that one of the cowboys was a Negro. "He plays and wrestles with the others on a footing of perfect equality," the Baron said. "It is very curious."

There were exceptions, of course, to the kind of "perfect equality" that so surprised the Baron. Sometimes Negro cowboys were forced to do the roughest and dirtiest work of trail and ranch. Like one cowboy known only as Negro John, they resented such treatment.

John was hired in Dodge City by a large outfit driving 4,800 steers north from Texas. The old cook had left the drive, and John was to replace him. As the drive moved north, John proved to be an excellent cowboy but a miserable cook. He was the best roper in the outfit, but his cooking left everybody hungry and unhappy.

"With him," one cowboy complained, "we got nothing to eat."

By the time the crew got to South Dakota, they had run out of food and John was cooking nothing but coffee. The cowboys had to beg meals and supplies from other outfits they met on the trail.

When they finally delivered their steers to the Warren and Guiterman ranch, the trail crew got their first good meal in weeks. They agreed to stay on a few days and help with the branding of the herd.

Although John was admitted to be the best roper in the crew, he was not allowed to do the roping. He had to give place to a white man who complained that no Negro could sit above him on a horse. So John worked on foot in the heat and dust of the corral, wrestling and branding steers, while the white man did a sloppy job of roping the cattle.

When the job was done, the crew took baths in the creek, put on clean clothes, and started for home. At noon they stopped to rest their horses, ate a meal of bread and bacon, and lay down for a nap. While they slept, John took some food and left for good.

He also took two things from the man who had replaced him as a roper. To show his resentment, he stole the other cowboy's Bible and dictionary. He probably did not keep them very long, though. Like many other ex-slaves, John did not know how to read!

Unlike John, some Negro cowboys stayed at the end of the trail in South Dakota. A few worked as horsebreakers, and others became ranch hands. One named Bunk White, for instance, became the only cowboy employed on a small ranch run by Bill Benoist. He rode long hours on Benoist's range and on the Indian reservation land that Benoist liked to use for his cattle.

He also was sent "to rep" for Benoist's W B Bar brand whenever there was a roundup in the area. "To rep" meant to represent his outfit. Whenever Bunk White found steers with the W B Bar brand on them, he cut them out of the roundup herd and drove them back to Benoist's range—sometimes making a trip of twenty miles or more.

But a twenty-mile drive was tame for a cowboy who had ridden the hundreds of miles from southern Texas to the Dakota Territory. The work was monotonous, and the winters were cold. Is is no wonder, then, that most of the cowboys who pioneered the trails through Oklahoma, Kansas, Nebraska, and South Dakota, eventually drew their pay and rode back to their home range in Texas.

Bose Ikard and the Goodnight-Loving Trail

✳ɕʌ One cattle trail out of Texas was entirely different from the trails that went north through Kansas. It went southwest through central Texas to the Pecos River, and then it turned north to go through New Mexico, Colorado, and Wyoming. Instead of running through rolling plains dotted by jack oaks and crossed by many rivers, it led through waterless deserts and over rough mountains. Instead of passing settled country and comparatively peaceful Indian reservations, it went through desolate wasteland menaced by hostile Comanches and Apaches.

It was pioneered by Colonel Charles Goodnight and Oliver Loving, two Texas cattlemen. Immediately after the end of the Civil War, these two men decided to drive their cattle to the army posts of New Mexico and the mining camps of Colorado. They threw their two herds together and began a drive from Weatherford, Texas.

There were various kinds of dangers on all the trails in those days. On the Goodnight-Loving Trail, however, there was a particular horror. Just before the trail reached the Pecos River, it had to go through about eighty miles of waterless desert.

On the trail a longhorn herd normally needed water every day. In an emergency it could go two days without water, but thirst was hard on a steer. It did not like going without water, so it became unruly and hard to handle. Goodnight and Loving knew that to get across the eighty miles of desert the herd would have to go approximately five days without water. The cowboys had a problem.

On the first drive Goodnight and Loving started with a mixed herd that contained cows as well as steers. They realized that they had to move fast and that they could not be slowed down by calves born along the way. So each morning a cowboy had to shoot the calves born during the night. This unfortunate job fell to a Negro cowboy, Jim Fowler. Jim did not like the job, but he could not get out of it.

When the herd approached the long stretch of desert, Goodnight and Loving stopped at the headwaters of the Middle Concho. There they allowed the herd to drink its fill of fresh water and prepare for the long dry stretch ahead.

As they entered the desert, the trail bosses tried to pace the restless herd. They drove late in the afternoon and in the early morning, hoping to save the strength of the cattle. But the thirsty, restless animals would not bed down at night; they merely milled around. So the cowboys found it easier to drive straight through.

Texas longhorns are driven north over the Chisholm Trail. Painting by W. H. Jackson.

George Glenn, who rode the Chisholm Trail in 1870.

Jim Beckworth, one of the most famous of the mountain men, ranged over wide areas of the Rocky Mountains.

Negro miner in Auburn Ravine in 1852, during the California gold rush.

White and Negro miners worked many claims together during the early days of California gold mining. This daguerreotype was taken in Spanish Flat in 1852.

Dodge City was the end of the trail for many cattle drives in the 1870's. Among the customers for clothing, cigars, and whiskey were hundreds of Negro cowboys.

Ben Hodges, a notorious cattle thief and confidence man, was one of the Negro cowboys who came with a Texas trail crew to Dodge City, where he lived until his death in 1929.

Nat Love claimed to have won the title of "Deadwood Dick" in a roping contest in Deadwood, South Dakota, in 1876. This photograph is from his autobiography, privately printed in 1907.

Frederic Remington often expressed admiration for Negro cavalrymen. Here his pen caught a trooper conversing in sign language with an Indian.

The band and four companies of the 25th colored infantry guarding Indian prisoners of war.

Jockey Oliver Lewis rode Aristides to win the first Kentucky Derby in 1875.

Second Lieutenant Henry Flipper was the first Negro officer to be graduated from West Point.

Joe Woods, "Nigger Jeff," Frank Drew, Hi Hatch, and Albert Potter who were together in the fight at St. Johns, Arizona.

Thornt Biggs helped his employer to become a millionaire stockman. He acted as pick-up man at the Albany County Fair and is shown here watching a hard-bucking horse being saddled.

Bronco Sam sometimes rode a mule while working for John Alsop on his ranch out on the Big Laramie River, about eight miles from Laramie City.

When Frederic Remington published his book *Pony Tracks* in 1895, he printed this picture of a Negro trail cook.

Shoshone Indians at Reno, Nevada, with "One Horse Charley," a noted Negro cowboy, photographed in 1886.

In 1902 Jimmy Winkfield was the last Negro jockey to win a Kentucky Derby.

Jim Perry; cook, fiddler, and all-round cowboy.

Mary Fields, photographed with shotgun in the late 1880's, ran a stage coach and mail route.

At the right of this group of XIT riders crossing the ferry at Fallon, Montana, is Newt Clendenen, known as "Nigger Newt."

After leaving the employ of the XIT, Bob Leavitt ran a saloon near Miles City, Montana, using his nickname "Nigger Bob" in his business, as shown on the sign here.

Bill Pickett, the famous bulldogger, on his horse
Spradley.

"Nigger Bob" Leavitt worked for the XIT during its
early years in Montana.

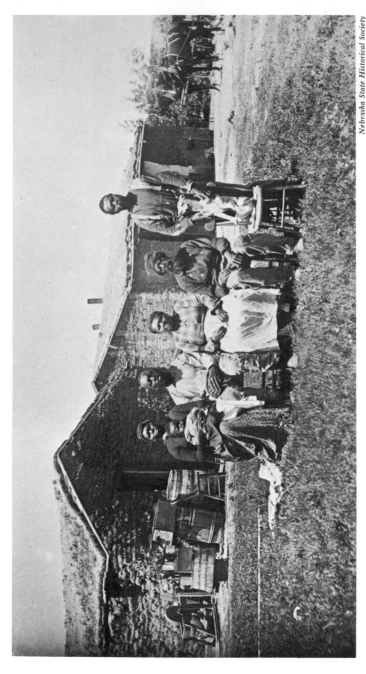

The sod home of the Shores family, who later became well-known as musicians, was typical of those erected by early settlers on the Nebraska frontier. This picture was taken in Custer County about the year 1887.

Goodnight led the way, guiding the point riders. Loving stayed with the drag, saving every animal he could. They lost some cattle on the drive across the desert stretch, those who could not survive without water. They lost more at the river, where about five hundred head stampeded after smelling the water of the Pecos. And they lost a few more to the poisoned alkali water of potholes that lined the trail.

That first drive over the Goodnight-Loving Trail made history in the cattle country. One of the cowboys who helped to make that history was Bose Ikard, a Negro. When the old cowboy died in Texas in 1929, the saddened Goodnight—a short time before his own death—erected a marker:

Bose Ikard

Served with me four years on the Goodnight-Loving Trail, never shirked a duty or disobeyed an order, rode with me in many stampedes, participated in three engagements with Comanches, splendid behavior.

C. Goodnight

Bose was born a slave in Mississippi before the Civil War. He was brought to Texas by his master's family, the Ikards, when he was five years old. Growing up on the frontier near Weatherford, Texas, he learned to ride, rope, and fight. These skills made him a valuable hand later.

Bose Ikard first rode for Oliver Loving. But when Loving died after a fight with Comanches, Bose began to ride for Goodnight. (J. Evetts Haley told the story in his fine book, *Charles Goodnight: Cowman and Plainsman*.)

Goodnight said that Bose "surpassed any man I had in endurance and stamina. There was a dignity, a cleanliness, and a reliability about him that was wonderful. He paid no attention to women. His behavior was very good in a fight, and he was probably the most devoted man to me that I ever had. I have trusted him farther than any living man. He was my detective, banker, and everything else in Colorado, New Mexico, and the other wild country I was in. The nearest and only bank was at Denver, and when we carried money I gave it to Bose, for a thief would never think of robbing him—never think of looking in a Negro's bed for money.

"We went through some terrible trials during those four years on the trail. While I had a good constitution and endurance, after being in the saddle for several days and nights at a time, on various occasions, and finding that I could stand it no longer, I would ask Bose if he would take my place, and he never failed to answer me in the most cheerful and willing manner, and was the most skilled and trustworthy man I had."

It would take many pages to tell about all the trails that Bose Ikard and Charles Goodnight rode together. J. Evetts Haley wrote that Bose Ikard "added life, friendship, and color to the Goodnight Trail. . . . To the end of his long days Goodnight subscribed his greatest debt to man still due this Negro who saved his life several times, this superb rider, remarkable trail hand, and devoted servant."

One time on the trail, just before dawn, there was a stampede. Because the cattle had been quiet, Goodnight had left Bose alone with the herd and had ridden in to the wagon to wake the cook and get the crew moving. Suddenly something startled the cattle, which came stampeding down toward the camp.

Goodnight grabbed a blanket and ran out waving it and

making as much noise as he could. In this way he was able to split the herd, which poured around the chuck wagon and the men sleeping on the ground. Then he found his horse, which was still tethered to the wagon wheel. He mounted and raced up the side of the stampeding herd.

By now dawn was near and Goodnight could see. Near the front flank of the herd he saw Bose, and in a few minutes Bose looked back, saw him, and immediately moved in to turn the leaders. Working together, the two men soon had the herd circled and the stampede stopped.

After things quieted down, Goodnight asked Bose why he had not tried to turn the herd earlier. Bose's explanation was simple: he had ridden flank near the front until he could see, for he had been afraid that Indians might be riding at the rear. Bose had a right to be worried, for stampeding trail herds was a favorite Comanche trick.

Bose Ikard showed a proper respect for Indians, but he was no coward. When Goodnight was injured in northern New Mexico and lay helpless in the shade of the wagon, Bose rode out to stop a local outlaw leader from cutting the herd. At the end of one drive, when Goodnight drove from Colorado to Texas carrying all the profits of the year's drives with him, Bose was in the driver's seat, armed and alert. He drove through a country made dangerous by outlaws, Indians, and lawless Mexicans.

Where the Goodnight-Loving Trail went north through New Mexico, it passed near Lincoln, the scene of the famous Lincoln County War. One of the main reasons this war became famous was that Billy the Kid took part in it. There are so many different stories about the Lincoln

County War that we will probably never know all of what actually happened.

Yet one thing is clear. In this bloody feud, both whites and Negroes died. Negroes fought on both sides, and Billy the Kid rode with Negroes. When the Kid and his gang were trapped in a burning building, Negroes were with them. Outside Negro troops surrounded the house. When Territorial Governor Lew Wallace (author of *Ben Hur*) searched for witnesses, trying to learn the truth about the madness in Lincoln County, he sent a Negro rider to find Billy the Kid and offer him safe conduct.

There were many cowboys who rode along the Goodnight-Loving Trail in New Mexico without getting into range feuds or getting their names in the newspapers. One of these, a Negro cowboy named Add, was range boss of the LFD outfit. Add usually headed a crew of south Texas Negro cowboys. According to Howard Thorp, himself a cowboy, songwriter, and ballad collector, Add was one of the best cowhands on the Pecos River: "Cowmen from Tozah, Texas, to Las Vegas, New Mexico, knew Add, and many of them at different times had worked on roundups with him."

Experience as a range boss made Add an expert. He became famous among the cattlemen of the Southwest and eventually became the subject of a cowboy song. According to Howard Thorp, the song "concerns a critter found in one roundup and claimed by no one. Add was a dictionary on earmarks and brands, but this one was a puzzler even to him. He read the tally of the brands:

> She's got O Block an' Lightnin' Rod,
> Nine Forty-Six an' A Bar Eleven,
> Rafter Cross an'de double prod,

> Terrapin an' Ninety-Seven;
> Half Circle A an' Diamond D,
> Four-Cross L an' Three PZ;
> BWL, Bar XVV
> Bar N Cross an' ALC.

"Since none of the punchers claimed the critter, Old Add just added his own brand—'For one more brand or less won't do no harm.' "

Add was known and respected all over the Pecos area of New Mexico. So it was not surprising that the news of his plans spread rapidly when he told a few friends one fall that he intended to be married on Christmas day. Widely separated ranchers, all of whom knew and liked him, decided to send presents. Most of them, prompted by their practical wives, decided on the same present. So when Add and his bride rode on their wedding day to the Roswell freight depot, they found nineteen cookstoves waiting for them.

Cowboys like Bose and Add rode up all the trails. Their job was to deliver beef to a nation of hungry people. Through cloudbursts and burning sun, through mud and choking dust, these men rode on. They went where the trails went, and they did their jobs.

✳️ CHAPTER 8

Famous Dodge City

✳️ One night in Dodge City, when cattlemen, cowboys, muleskinners, and horsetraders jammed the streets, a tenderfoot lay sleeping in his hotel room. He had just arrived from the state of Indiana, and he was tired.

He woke with a start when he heard a loud banging on his door. Frightened but curious, he went to open it.

He saw an old man wearing two guns and a long black coat. Behind the old gentleman stood a Negro—so big that he looked like a giant.

"My name is Colonel Draper," the old man said. "The hotel is full, but the clerk said you might share your room with us."

The tenderfoot was uncertain. He stared for a moment at the Colonel and his giant companion. Then he invited them in.

The old man took off his coat and guns and hung them on the back of a chair. The Negro spread a blanket on the floor and put a paper parcel down beside it.

"Now don't you mind Zeke," the old man said. "I brought him along to guard that parcel."

"What's in it?" the tenderfoot asked.

"Five thousand dollars wrapped in that paper. Going to buy a herd of cattle tomorrow when they come in," the Colonel answered.

Zeke lay down on the blanket, took a long knife from inside his shirt and stuck it into the jamb of the door. Then he took out another knife and drove it into the floor, within easy reach.

So guarded, the tenderfoot and the Colonel spent a quiet night in Dodge City. Down on the street below them, however, activity and noise continued far into the night. There cattlemen, cowboys, buffalo hunters, and muleskinners crowded the wooden walks and saloons. Some stood at the bars, drinking raw whiskey. Others sat at the gambling tables playing poker, drawing cards which each hoped would change his luck and make him a fortune. Some spent their time with the dance-hall girls, dancing to music played on an old piano.

Dodge was a typical cowtown. It was a cattle market, a place where cattlemen came to buy stock for the northern ranges of Nebraska, Montana, and the Dakotas. It was also a shipping point where men loaded tens of thousands of Texas cattle on railroad cars and sent them back to markets in Kansas City or Chicago. It was the end of the trail for crews that drove north from Texas up through the Panhandle or the Indian Territory.

Dodge City was only one of the many early Kansas cowtowns. Abilene was the first, and Ellsworth, Newton, and Wichita also received thousands of cattle and went through brief periods of gaudy prosperity. Dodge City became the best known of them all because its cattle trade lasted for many years and because it attracted some of the most famous men in the West. Wyatt Earp and Bat Masterson, for instance, were two of its deputy marshals.

Earp and Masterson, together with other deputies like them, tried to maintain law and order among Texas cowboys, tough muleskinners, and hardened gamblers. The town council passed a law forbidding the carrying of guns in Dodge, and the marshals were usually successful in enforcing it. But sometimes they failed.

Henry Hilton, for instance, was a Negro who owned a ranch and ran a small herd of cattle near Dodge City. One day as he rode into town with a bunch of white cowboys, some began to torment him. When one of them tried to lasso him, Hilton said that he would not stand for any hazing. When the cowboy persisted, throwing a loop and nearly pulling Hilton off his horse, the Negro drew his gun and shot his tormenter. About half of the cowboys believed that Hilton was justified.

"It was self-defense," they said.

Two other Negroes had a fight that made more noise but stopped short of killing. They were bullwhackers who drove big freight wagons, and their weapons were bull whips. They were experts, and in their hands the whips were deadly. With a twelve-foot whip, a bullwhacker could reach the ear of a lead ox or mule, and with equal accuracy he could flick a cigar from a man's mouth. He could tear a gun from a man's hand, the clothing from his body, or the flesh from his bones.

So when the two bullwhackers fought in the middle of the

main street of Dodge City, they quickly drew a crowd. The snapping of their whips sounded like pistol shots, and every stroke cut deep into flesh. One of the crowd described the action briefly: "Blood flowed and dust flew and the crowd cheered until Policeman Joe Mason came along and suspended the cheerful exercise."

Negroes suffered from some discrimination in Dodge City, but most of them rode with white friends and were supported by white bosses. There were many white cattlemen like Jim Thornhill, for instance.

"Jim had a code of his own," one of his friends said. "I knew his affection for his boys, yet I have heard Jim say he would rather see any of his boys dead than ever take a backstep when they knew they were in the right.

"Jim held no racial prejudice. Black, white, yellow, and red, they were all alike to Jim. Only the individual counted, no matter what his color or creed—and a friend could do no wrong."

Jim Thornhill was lucky that Ben Hodges was not one of his friends. For Ben was an expert at doing wrong. He was a thorough rascal and confidence man. He was also a competent forger and cattle thief.

The son of a Negro father and a Mexican mother, Ben Hodges came up the trail from Texas with one of the first herds to arrive in Dodge City. He was unlike the other men in his crew: they rode back to Texas, but he stayed in Dodge. There he talked his way into and out of trouble, stealing money and cattle, sometimes worrying and sometimes amusing the townspeople.

When he first rode into town, he heard a common rumor that much of the range land around Dodge City was a part of an old Spanish land grant. He immediately let it be known that he came from an old Spanish family and that he could claim ownership of the land.

He made a quick trip to Texas and returned with a set of papers that were supposed to prove his claim. He found a local lawyer who was willing to help him. The fact that Ben had no money did not hinder his progress. He was so persuasive and seemed so honest that many strangers in town were willing to help him. Even many old-timers who doubted him were willing to give him money and support, for they enjoyed watching the game.

Other cowboys who had ridden with Ben picked up his story and pushed it. They helped him find a Kansas City judge who joined in his legal actions. They were amused by watching him get credit from many local storekeepers. He rode an expensive saddle, wore a beautiful set of spurs, and carried a fine gun. The town watched him and helped him because the show was worth the price.

After he had won local fame by claiming ownership of the land grant, he turned to other swindles. He got copies of the tax bills for twenty thousand acres of unsettled Kansas range, copies that anyone could get by writing to the proper county clerk. Then he waited for an opportunity to use them.

The opportunity came when a disastrous fire gutted the Wright and Beverly General Store and dropped the store's four-ton safe into the basement. The safe fell on its doors, and for a while its contents were securely out of circulation.

Ben acted promptly. He took his tax bills and visited the president of the Dodge City National Bank. He knew that

the banker was a newcomer in town, a man who had no reason to doubt his word.

Ben produced the tax bills and said that he owned the
twenty thousand acres of Kansas range land. He added that
his deeds for the land were temporarily locked in the Wright
and Beverly safe. He talked so fast and so well that the
banker wrote him a letter stating that Ben was known to
be the owner of thirty-two sections in Kansas.

Then Ben took the banker's letter and used it to get
other letters that confirmed his ownership of the land and
his reputation for honesty.

With all this "evidence" to prove that he was a wealthy
man, Ben suddenly left Dodge City. He rode south to meet
the trail crews coming up across Beaver Creek and the Cimarron River. He talked with the bosses and owners and
contracted for spring delivery of thousands of cattle. Then
he rode back to Dodge.

Now he tried to borrow money from bankers. The price
of cattle rose steadily, and it looked as if he would make a
large profit on the cattle he had "bought."

Then he learned that all bankers, Eastern and Western,
were far more careful about lending money than about
writing letters of recommendation. They asked for real
proof of his land ownership, and none of his fast talking
worked. So all of his cattle deals fell through.

He was more successful with smaller swindles. He got
free passes from the railroads every year because he per-
suaded them that he was a large owner and shipper of cattle. And he could always make a few dollars.

One of his swindles was made possible by bad weather.
Two cattlemen who were partners drove thousands of cat-

tle up the trail and held them on the range south of Dodge City. Then spring storms stampeded their herds and scattered their horses, cows, and steers over several counties.

Because the two cattlemen had many business responsibilities, they had to leave Dodge City before all their herds had been rounded up. So they left an agent to receive stray cattle and horses as they were recovered. The agent offered to pay a dollar a head for their cattle and two dollars for their horses. He paid with receipts which were to be redeemed by Major Conklin, one of the partners. Conklin was now in Kansas City.

Ben Hodges immediately saw the weakness of this system of doing business. He visited Major Conklin in Kansas City and presented forged receipts for several hundred cattle and horses.

Conklin did not question the receipts, which seemed to be in order, but he decided that he could drive a hard bargain with a poor and ignorant Negro cowboy. So he offered Ben less than the value of the receipts and finally settled by paying for Ben's room and board, buying him a complete new outfit, and giving him about sixty dollars.

When Conklin's partner, John Lytle, returned to Kansas City, Conklin met him at the bar of the St. James Hotel. A number of other cattlemen were with them, drinking and talking, when Conklin boasted of his bargain.

"John," he said, producing the forged receipts, "I made a shrewd business deal and got the receipts for several hundred cattle and horses for less than half price. I got them from a cowboy named Ben Hodges. . . ."

He was interrupted by loud laughter. All the other cattlemen knew Ben, and they knew that the receipts must be forgeries. Ben had pulled a perfect swindle, for Major Conklin was hardly eager to enter a court and describe his "shrewdness" in bargaining with a poor cowhand. It was better to accept the loss.

Sometimes, however, Ben did get arrested. Once when the whole herd of a local dairyman was stolen, Ben was charged with the crime. The circumstantial evidence was strong, and he seemed certain to be convicted. He had only a few real friends, no money, and a bad reputation. He had no lawyer.

Ben pleaded his own case. After all the evidence had been presented, he rose to address the jury. He talked for more than two hours, sometimes making them laugh, sometimes becoming serious or indignant.

"What! Me?" he cried at one point, "the descendant of old grandees of Spain, the owner of a land grant embracing millions of acres, the owner of gold mines and villages and towns situated on that grant of which I am sole owner, to steal a miserable, miserly lot of old cows? Why, the idea is absurd. No, gentlemen, I think too much of the race of men from which I sprang, to disgrace their memory."

At another point, forgetting all about his claims to gold and towns and cities, he represented himself as a poor but honest cowboy being accused by personal enemies. At all times he was persuasive, bewildering, and entertaining. When he finished his pleading, he won his case. The jury brought in a verdict of not guilty.

A few days later the missing cows came home. Their tracks told the whole story. Ben had indeed stolen them and driven them some fifty miles to a hidden canyon. He had left them unguarded, and a storm had started them moving. Fortunately for Ben, they returned after he had been acquitted.

Adventures like this made Ben famous in Dodge City. Everybody knew him, though few people trusted him. But Ben did not worry, and he was full of new ideas.

He next decided to become a livestock inspector. He petitioned the governor for the job, saying that he had always been a good, hard-working Republican. He supported his petition with the signatures of local saloon-keepers, cowboys, gamblers, and dance-hall girls. They found the idea amusing.

Not so the town's businessmen and cattlemen. They said that Ben's asking to be a livestock inspector was "like a wolf asking to guard the sheep pen." They informed the governor that Ben was one of the country's most competent cattle thieves, and his petition was rejected. Barred from a career as a state employee, Ben continued his life as a shifty citizen.

He outlived almost all his friends and enemies. He grew to be a very old man, and he shuffled painfully along the changing streets of Dodge City. Sometimes he carried an empty six-shooter, now so dirty and rusted it could not be fired. Children followed him to hear his stories, and he became a kind of living legend.

By 1929, when Ben died and was buried in the Maple Grove Cemetery, many of the old-time cattlemen and cowboys had preceded him. His grave was near theirs.

"We buried Ben there for a good reason," one of his pallbearers said. "We wanted him where they could keep an eye on him."

Even in death, Ben Hodges was a lucky man. He had

lived through Dodge City's most exciting times. He had been a notorious rascal during the days when Wyatt Earp had patrolled the dance halls and saloons. And he lived on to see Fords and Chevrolets parked thickly on the city streets. When he died he found a secure resting place among the founding fathers of the town.

Dodge City itself, for that matter, eventually ceased to be a cowtown. As railroads were built across the country and south into Texas, the old trail drives ended. Dodge City became a market center for Kansas wheat farmers and ranchers; and schools and churches replaced the old saloons and dance halls.

✳︎ᛒ CHAPTER **9**

Cowboys and Cowtowns

✳︎ᛒ Dodge City became known as the Queen of the Cowtowns, but other places in the old West were almost as famous as Dodge. Deadwood, South Dakota, for example, was once a wide-open town full of miners and cowboys. But soon the Dakota ranges were stocked with their own cattle, and most of the little mining claims were exhausted. Then Deadwood became a quiet place. Today it is known as the home of America's biggest gold-mining company, and it is famed for its quiet streets, excellent schools, and modern hospitals.

Yet Deadwood has its memories of wilder days. It remembers the crews of white and Negro cowboys who rode yelling through the streets and the troops of white and Negro cavalry who rode in from Fort Meade to spend their pay. It remembers how Wild Bill Hickok died in a Deadwood saloon, shot in the back as he held a poker hand of aces and eights. Since then a hand which has two aces and two eights has been known as a "dead man's hand."

Other old cowtowns have famous names. Deep in the Southwest, drowsing in the sun of the high Arizona desert, Tombstone now lives on memories and tourists. The tourists listen to the old stories of the fight at the O. K. Corral, where Doc Holiday, the Earps, and the Clantons met and fought. The tourists walk through Boot Hill, where many old-time gunmen are buried: Charley Storms, shot by Luke Short, 1880; Marshal White, shot by Curly Bill, 1880; Red River Tom, shot by Ormsby, 1882. One of the Negroes buried in Boot Hill was Delia William, the proprietress of a lodging house on Toughnut Street.

Sometimes the tourists hear the stories told about Jim and Bat, two of the first Negro cowboys in the Arizona Territory.

Jim was a near giant of a man who rode for John H. Slaughter. He came with Slaughter's trail drives from Maverick, Texas, through New Mexico to Arizona. There he helped his employer build and hold a great cattle ranch.

As a cowboy and as a miner, Jim soon proved his courage and determination. He had strength to match his size and he was afraid of nothing. When Frank Leslie, notorious as one of Tombstone's killers, tried to steal a mining claim that Jim had staked, Jim ran him off. Jim could not be bluffed.

Once, however, his strength and nerve merely earned him a beating. The great heavyweight champion John L. Sullivan came to Tombstone and offered five hundred dollars to any man who could fight him for two rounds. Jim accepted the challenge, and the match was held.

When the two men stepped out on the stage, the giant Negro cowboy towered over his opponent. Sullivan looked like a runt by comparison. The audience, mostly miners and cowboys, cheered for Jim.

The bell sounded. Jim began with a looping roundhouse swing that caught Sullivan high on the head and threw him off balance. The audience cheered again.

That was their last cheer. Jim had strength, but no science. The great John L. Sullivan was a veteran boxer, and it took him only a few seconds to end Jim's ring career. The cowboy was carried out feet first.

He woke up with a headache. When he was interviewed the next day by the Tombstone newspaper, he said that he must have been doped, for he was still "feeling dopey."

Nobody else in Tombstone agreed with him. Having seen what Sullivan's famous right hand could do, all the local citizens were impressed. When Sullivan offered to fight the four biggest men in Tombstone all at once, nobody volunteered. When the world champion boasted that he could knock out a mule with one punch, nobody produced an expensive mule for the sacrifice. Tombstone had already offered its best in Jim.

Jim remained in Tombstone, settling down and occasionally swapping stories about his early days in the territory. He told tales of eighty-mile cattle drives across waterless deserts, and he remembered many of the more exciting adventures of John Slaughter's move into the Arizona Territory. He remembered, too, that he had not been Slaughter's only Negro cowboy.

One of the others was known only as Bat. Once Bat accompanied Slaughter and his foreman into Mexico on a dangerous cattle-buying expedition. There the three of them were attacked by a good-sized bunch of Mexican bandits near Montezuma. The three men fought off the bandits and returned to Tombstone without loss.

Still other Negro cowboys rode for ranchers in the northern part of Arizona. Near the little town of St. Johns, for instance, a Texas family named Greer built a large horse-and-cattle ranch and competed for land and water with their Mexican neighbors. Almost immediately their competition became open conflict. First the Greers' cattle were stampeded and scattered. Then the Greer crews rode against the Mexican sheep camps, shooting and scattering flocks. Soon the conflict was a grudge feud, a bitter range war.

Once Dick Greer and his crew were nearly trapped in the town of St. Johns itself. Surrounded by armed Mexicans, Greer and his cowboys retreated toward their horses. When the shooting started, most of the crew took shelter in an empty adobe house, but three of the cowboys reached their horses and made their escape. One of these was a Negro, a cowboy named Jeff who covered their rear, standing off pursuers while the other two got away. Then he made his escape, although he was wounded in a long running fight that covered the many miles between St. Johns and the rugged Dry Lakes Country.

The cowboys who were trapped in the adobe house held off their attackers and survived a long siege. Eventually they were freed by other cowboys, and returned to their ranch.

The range war continued for many months, and Jeff was one of the Negro cowboys who fought in it. Yet Jeff might not be remembered as a Negro if he had not posed with a group of his friends in a local photographic studio. Otherwise he probably would be known only as a brave cowboy who rode through a big crowd of threatening Mexicans, fighting a rear guard action against nearly hopeless odds and helping to save the lives of two of his friends.

Most of the thousands of cowboys who rode through cow-towns of the West are now nameless and forgotten. They drove cattle, crossed rivers, got sick on alkali water or bad whiskey, and retired young. But they rarely made the papers, fought in bloody range wars, or were named or described in memories of old cattlemen. The name of a cowboy usually appeared in Western newspapers only if he was engaged in murder, theft, or riot.

The earliest records of Denver, Colorado, are typical. The newspapers specialized in the violent and the unusual. Therefore many of the miners and cowboys they described were tough characters. Thus Dan Diamond, one of the "worst" Negro cowboys ever to come to Denver, made headlines in the early 1870's. He participated in a group escape from the county jail. He broke out, stole a horse, and rode more than twenty-four miles down the South Platte River before being recaptured by a posse.

Ten years later, when a disguised detective was mistakenly arrested and thrown into the Denver jail, he remarked that "it contained about twenty of the worst specimens of humanity, both black and white, that it was ever my misfortune to be housed with in one small room." Two years later Andy Green, "a Negro tough" who had been convicted of the murder of a horse-car driver, was the last man to be hanged publicly in Denver.

Most of the Negroes in Denver were quiet and peaceful men. Many worked in the stockyards which stretched several miles from the center of town along the South Platte

River. Others worked in mines like the Robert E. Lee at Leadville, where $118,500 in silver was mined in one day. Still others worked in saloons: when the little town of Robinson, near Leadville, opened its first school, one of its students was a ten-year-old Negro girl named Pearl. She went to school during the day and sang in a dance hall at night.

Many Negro cowboys rode into or through Denver as members of Texas trail crews. As new Colorado ranges opened up, some stayed to become permanent settlers. Several cattlemen later wrote of knowing Negroes "who made extra good cowhands."

One who proved his ability in the day-to-day work of trail and range was Thornton Biggs, who worked for Ora Haley's Two Bar Ranch. The Two Bar brand became a symbol of the best in ranching on the Colorado and Wyoming ranges. According to one report, "Haley's success in the cattle business was due to a long-time employee, a Negro named Thornton (Thornt) Biggs. During an eventful life he won the reputation of being the best top hand ever to fork a bronc or doctor a sick cow on the Laramie Plains. Although he never became a range manager or even a foreman, he taught a whole generation of future range managers, wagon bosses, and all-round cowpunchers the finer points of the range cattle business.

"Thornt was no angel. He shot craps and hit the bottle occasionally. But that is neither here nor there. Thornt Biggs was one of a small group of dedicated men without whose loyal support and technical know-how Ora Haley never would have made the fortune he did."

During his last years Thornt Biggs worked in Cheyenne,

Wyoming. By then the center of the cattle business had moved north. Although Colorado always remained an important stock-raising territory, its grazing lands were limited by comparison with the fifty million acres of unfenced land in Wyoming. The capital of this new cattle empire was Cheyenne—a shipping point, market, and meeting place for cattlemen and cowboys.

In this booming cowtown the finest hotel was owned and operated by B. M. Ford, a Negro. His Ford House was almost always crowded, and frequently he had to turn guests away. Thus when John Meldrum came from New York to Cheyenne with his new bride and a small wedding party, he found the hotel full. For a while he pled and argued without any result. Then, as he later remembered, "The landlord finally said he could give us one room. That was the best he could do. I told him to give the girls the room and we would go out and rustle. He told us that he had lots of floor space in the office, lots of rugs and buffalo robes, but no beds. We spent the night in the office and were packed in like sardines. When you wanted to turn over you had to holler 'spoon.' Thas was how I spent my first night in Cheyenne."

When his first hotel burned down, Ford built a new one, "a fine modern three-story structure." Ford's Inter Ocean Hotel was said to be one of the best in the West, "fully equal to the Grand Central in Omaha." It housed a wide variety of guests during colorful times. One was a bridegroom who wore a high silk hat, but who gave it up when he was told that someone would shoot it off his head if he tried to wear it on the streets in Cheyenne. Another was Indian Chief Spotted Tail, who predicted the battle of the

Little Bighorn weeks before Custer was defeated and killed. One was Captain Pollock of the 9th Infantry, who met his death by falling down the hotel stairs.

Other guests, like those who stayed in the hotel during a five-day blizzard in March, 1878, were grateful for its three-story magnificence. They "walked out of second story windows on top of the drifts."

B. M. Ford's Inter Ocean Hotel was the center of the town's social life in Cheyenne's earliest days. There seems to have been comparatively little anti-Negro prejudice in Wyoming. Cheyenne's first school, for instance, was built at the same time as the Ford House and dedicated on January 5, 1868. The "best citizens" gathered there for the dedication, crowding together while the thermometer outside dropped to twenty-three degrees below zero. They were proud of having established a school that would be open to all, "rich or poor, black or white." Ten years later, Cheyenne continued to show the same disregard for most racial and religious differences: "The Catholics held fairs and festivals to raise money for church work. The Ladies Sewing Society of the Congregational Church sewed for the needy. Jewish residents celebrated Yom Kippur with much ceremony. Colored voters organized a political club and nominated one of their members, W. J. Hardin, a popular barber, to the territorial legislature. Hardin was elected and served with credit." Even today, when students of the nearby University of Wyoming sing their college song, they boast:

> . . . the college throws its portals
> Open wide to all men free.

The opening of the Wyoming cattle country resulted in continual fighting with Indians, who tried to retain their old lands. The citizens of Cheyenne and Laramie knew that danger was always near, but foolish or unlucky settlers learned hard lessons. In 1876, for example, Charles Metz and his wife, accompanied only by Rachel Briggs, a Negro woman, were killed by Indians as they traveled on the road to Laramie. The Indians took Rachel Briggs prisoner, but when she tried to escape they killed her too. This happened the same year that General Custer and his men died at the Little Bighorn.

Yet Texas cowboys continued to drive great herds to the Wyoming ranges. Ab Blocker brought in a herd of 3,700 steers, using both white and Negro cowboys. His chuck wagon was drawn by oxen, and some extra work cattle were included in the drive. One of the oxen, an old animal named Bully, soon became a nuisance because he refused to leave the wagon. When he was not pulling it, he was following it, with his head right at the tailboard.

One of Blocker's Negro cowboys was able to use old Bully's love of the chuck wagon. When the outfit reached the Platte River, which was ice cold and running high, Blocker decided that he would have to drive the herd in and across. But the cowboy had a different idea. He suggested that they drive the herd up the river a few miles to an old government bridge. There they would start the chuck wagon across the bridge, but hold Bully with the lead steers on the near side.

Blocker tried the plan, and it worked. When the wagon was almost across the bridge, the cowboys let Bully go. He raced across the bridge after the wagon, and the lead steers went with him. The other steers followed them. More than three thousand cattle crossed the Platte River without wetting a hoof—and none of them had ever been on a bridge before!

Other large herds came to and through Wyoming as the plains were cleared of Indians and the open-range cattle business boomed. Attracted by stories of fat profits, foreign investors helped to organize cattle companies controlling thousands of acres of rangeland. And Cheyenne became a financial and social center for the cattle business.

At one time it was said to be the richest little city in the world. The Cheyenne Club was organized by wealthy cattlemen, and it became a center of power and luxury. Men and women came to the club to drink imported wines and eat fresh oysters. They dined and danced in formal dress. Cowboys who stood on the sidewalks and watched their bosses parading by in starched white shirts and black coats called them Herefords—because they looked a little like black and white cattle.

For the cowboys themselves, pleasures were cheaper and simpler. Sometimes they were surprising.

Bill Walker described what his trail crew did when it stopped its herd in a canyon south of Cheyenne.

"Cheyenne had only one real street then," Walker said. "It had a clothing store with a plate-glass front, and that store front was the only mirror that a lot of those cowboys had ever looked into. That burg had plenty of saloons and poker joints, and they all got plumb fat and prosperous as soon as our bunch hit town."

Three days later Walker's bunch was back with its herd. The cowboys had lost a lot of money, and they were still a little drunk. So they planned one last fling, something to make the bartenders and gamblers of Cheyenne remember them.

One of the cowboys was Bronco Sam, a "genuine black buckaroo who wasn't afraid of anything and who could ride them all." The crew decided to rope the biggest longhorn in the herd, saddle it, and have the Negro bronc buster ride it through Cheyenne's main street. Bronco Sam liked the idea.

They roped and saddled the steer, and Sam mounted it. Then they rode toward Cheyenne, whooping and hollering and swinging knotted ropes to drive the bucking steer.

By the time the show got into town, Sam's mount was frantic. It was a frightened, wild-eyed steer, pitching and bawling.

When it saw itself reflected in the plate glass window of the clothing store, if stopped and pawed the ground. Then it took off and charged.

Right through the windows, down the aisles, over the counters, and around the shelves. Terrified sales clerks went diving into corners for protection while the steer plunged through the clothing racks.

Then it charged back out through the empty window frame.

According to Bill Walker, "Sam was still in the saddle, the steer's horns decorated with pants, coats, underwear, and other odds and ends of gearin'." The steer was still jumping as the cowboys closed in to drive him toward the herd. Sam was shouting that he had brought out a suit of clothes for everybody in the crew.

Sam and the other cowboys had sobered up by the time

they unsaddled the steer and turned it into the herd. Sam roped his horse, and they all rode back to town to face the music.

When they got there, the storekeepers gave them a cold reception. "But Sam was wise enough to act right," Walker said. "He was all smiles, good manners, and apologies, and he asked terrible polite what the damages might be. That was different. The store men got their books and tallied up, and when they told him the price—three hundred and fifty dollars—old Sam never even batted an eye. He just peeled it off in good old greenbacks and passed it over like he was donating." Then he and his crew rode out of Cheyenne.

But Sam came back. In later years he worked on ranches near Cheyenne and Laramie. He settled down somewhat, but he was still proud of his skill as a rider. He could ride anything—steers, horses, mules—as long as it had four legs and hair.

He again made a great stir—this time in Laramie—when he bet that he could ride his horse up the steep front stairs of the Frontier House, the best hotel in Laramie. He nearly did it, too, but then the stairs collapsed when Sam was half way up. He and his horse and a lot of lumber fell through to the basement.

Bronco Sam was in no way unusual. Other cowboys, both white and Negro, did as much to keep life in the cowtowns from getting dull. They rode their horses into saloons, shot holes in railroad water tanks, and got into good-natured wrestling matches that sometimes ended in the town watering trough or the marshal's jail. Most of them were young, unmarried, and happily irresponsible.

Towns like Cheyenne and Laramie survived their wildest days to become settled cities with libraries, museums, concert halls, and colleges. Other cowtowns grew up suddenly at the side of a railroad track or the end of a railroad spur. They became quiet little villages as the country settled down to farming and cattle raising on fenced ranches.

But even in the smallest towns of Montana, more than a thousand miles from the Texas plains, men remember the Texas crews that drove the wild longhorn cattle to the northern ranges. Typical of these crews was the first one that the Texas XIT Ranch sent north to its two-million-acre Montana ranch. Because the cattle came much of the way by rail, only seven cowboys were needed to drive them. Of these, one was a Negro. And one or two Negroes were usually a part of every crew that came after them.

Most of these cowboys delivered their cattle and rode back to Texas. But a few were like the Negro Bob Leavitt, who decided to stay in Montana. He worked on the XIT Montana range for a number of years and then opened his own saloon—a small log shack that stood by itself on an empty, windswept plain. It became the social center for cowboys from many widely separated, lonely ranches.

In little Montana towns, as in little towns throughout the West, there were always a few Negro women as well as Negro cowboys. Perhaps the most remarkable of these was Stagecoach Mary Fields, onetime nurse and servant to the Ursuline Sisters at St. Peter's Mission. She later became a restaurant owner, a freighter, a stagecoach driver and finally, when she was about seventy, a laundress in Cascade, Montana.

During her long life, Stagecoach Mary learned to use a

revolver and a shotgun, fought at least one gun duel, and developed a taste for hard liquor and black cigars.

Even when she was over seventy, she could still take direct action. One day she stopped in the local saloon for a shot of straight whiskey. Looking out the window, she saw a customer who had refused to pay his laundry bill. She followed him down the street, grabbed him by the collar, and knocked him down with her fist. Then she marched back to the saloon.

"His laundry bill is paid," she said.

Mustangers and Bronc Busters

✳︎ℭᴅ   Every spring thousands of people gather in Louisville, Kentucky, to watch the running of the Kentucky Derby. They come from Texas and California and from Maine and Florida. They crowd the old clubhouse and jam into the famous grandstand.

Neither the clubhouse nor the present grandstand had been built when the first Kentucky Derby was run in 1875, ten years after the end of the Civil War. But the mile-long oval, the white fence, and the flower-dotted bluegrass infield looked much as they do now. The crowd was large—nearly ten thousand people—and newspapers reported that the ladies who watched the race were a "dazzling array of feminine loveliness."

The horses paraded before the stands—more than a dozen thoroughbreds with gleaming coats. The crowd cheered them by name. Volcano and Aristides were favored, but there were backers for Chesapeake, Verdigris, Searcher, and Vagabond.

The jockeys cantered their horses on the backstretch and then headed for the starting line. Suddenly came the familiar cry, "They're off!" signalling the start of the first Derby. Volcano took the lead and held it for a half mile. Then Aristides—always known affectionately as "the little red horse"—took the lead and held it. The crowd screamed wildly when Aristides crossed the finish line the winner, running the mile and a half in 2 minutes, 37¾ seconds, a new record for a three-year-old horse.

Aristides' rider was Jockey Lewis, one of the thirteen Negro jockeys who rode in that first race at Churchill Downs. From then until 1902, Negroes won eleven of the Derbies. One of them, Isaac Murphy, was America's finest rider during the last two decades of the century, and he was the first jockey to win three Derbies.

It is not surprising that Negroes were good horsemen. Even as slaves they had always worked with horses. They were stableboys, trainers, and jockeys, and they did far more riding than most men in the North. Because the sticky clay of the South, until modern times, prevented the building of good roads, all men rode horseback. During the Civil War, white Southerners proved their horsemanship in the cavalry; after the War both white Southerners and Negroes showed their skill in the cavalry and on race tracks and open ranges.

Texas cowboys caught and broke many of their own horses. They went out on the range and searched for mustangs, wild horses that belonged to nobody. These were the descendants of the first horses brought to America by the Spanish. During hundreds of years of freedom on the

Texas plains they remained small and rough and shaggy, but they also became intelligent and tough.

Once caught and broken, these horses made perfect cow ponies. Without the speed and endurance of these captured mustangs, the cowboys would never have been able to round up nearly wild longhorns for long drives to market. At distances up to four hundred yards, the cow ponies were amazing. They could overtake anything else on four legs. Today their descendants are called quarter horses because they can start quickly and run a quarter of a mile in record time.

Catching wild mustangs was difficult. Imagine a herd of forty beautiful mares running wild on the Texas plains, led by a big fearless stallion. They were free, they ran very fast, and by instinct they stayed away from men. How could they be caught?

In the old days it was said that the men who went out after wild mustangs were "walking" them. Apparently the term "walking" came from the idea that Indians trailed wild horses on foot. There was also a story that a group of men going West to the California gold fields lost their horses and set out on foot to try to capture some wild mustangs. It is very doubtful, however, that any man on foot was ever able to walk down a wild horse.

Mustangs traveled in groups. The groups were made up of a herd of mares, each led by a stallion. Each herd stayed within its own area, a piece of land about twenty-five miles across. But each herd knew that piece of land as well as a child knows his own back yard or his neighborhood playground. The mustangs were very fast, and they knew where to run when someone was after them.

When a Texas rancher wanted a herd of mustangs, he

usually sent out two cowboys to bring them in. The cowboys followed the herd on horseback, changing their horses
frequently. The idea was that when the mustangs became
tired, they could be captured. The herd's success in out-
witting the mustangers (the name given to cowboys who
went after wild horses) depended on the stallion who led
them. He ordinarily led them at night, but he never took
them to the same place by the same route. At times he got
behind his herd and nipped chunks from the rumps of the
slow mares. At other times he fought another stallion—to
the death if necessary—who tried to move in and take over
his herd.

Catching the stallion was the trick the mustangers had
to learn, and they hoped to capture him alive. It was not
always possible, however, to catch a fast and clever stallion,
so in some cases the mustangers shot him. Once the stallion
was caught or killed it was not too difficult to capture his
mares because they then ran without a leader. If the mustangers were good enough, they could run down a herd of
wild horses in two weeks. Many times, though, the stallion
was too smart for the cowboys, and they would give up and
go back to the ranch with nothing.

Years ago there was a cowboy down in Texas named John
Young who set out to "walk down" a particular herd of
mustangs. The stallion, a beautiful sorrel, had thirty-five
mares in his herd. Helping John Young was a Negro named
Bill Nunn. The two men took turns walking the mustangs
(on horseback) for several days, until the herd looked nearly
exhausted and ready for capture. But at just that moment,
the wrong moment for John Young, his own horse dropped
dead from exhaustion.

Young was alone and on foot and many miles from any

kind of help. Like all cowboys, he wore tight-fitting boots and almost never walked. So by the time he got back to his temporary camp—many painful hours and several weary miles later—his feet were covered with dozens of blisters. He was so tired and discouraged that he gave all of his interest in the mustangs to his friend Bill Nunn. He was, he said, "through with mustangs forever."

Bill Nunn got a Mexican mustanger to help him, and they soon brought in the herd of wild horses, which they sold for a good price.

One of the most unusual of all the mustangers was a Negro named Bob Lemmons. One of the remarkable things about Bob was that he always mustanged alone. His methods were unique. Explaining them, he said, "I acted like I was a mustang. I made the mustangs think I was one of them."

Most mustangers followed a herd by trying to keep it in sight, but Bob Lemmons followed tracks. He learned the tracks of his herd so well that he could recognize the hoofprints of every horse in it. So even though his herd might mingle with another, or cross the tracks of still another, he was always close behind. He once trailed a group of mustangs for five days without actually seeing it.

When this unusual cowboy began to follow a herd of wild mustangs, he separated himself completely from all human contact. He changed neither his horse nor his clothing. His food was placed in a tree by other cowboys, and he did not pick it up until it had been there long enough to have lost its man-smell.

For a few days Bob Lemmons followed his mustangs at a distance, but then he gradually moved closer to them.

After he rode close to them for several days, they more or less got used to him and no longer noticed him. Finally they began to accept him as part of the group. Then Bob found an opportunity to drive off the stallion and begin to lead the mares himself. At this point he had not only become a mustang, he had become the stallion.

As the leader, Bob Lemmons won the confidence of the mares. He took them to water, and at times he kept them from going to water. He smelled for danger in a way they could understand. If a stallion came too close he drove it off. He led them in a flight, from fear; and he led them in a stampede. Gradually he took them onto new ranges, where he tested their confidence in him. In every way Bob Lemmons became a mustang, "except in not eating grass and in having the long, long thoughts that only a human can have."

When the band of mustangs was completely under control, Bob Lemmons slowly led them homeward. By this time the cowboys at the ranch were expecting Bob and his wild horses, so all was in readiness. The gates of the temporary corral were opened and Bob suddenly broke into a dead run, leading his herd into the pen. Bob Lemmons "actually became the leader of a band of wild horses that followed him into a pen as fresh as they had been when he first sighted them." Now it was up to the cowboys to take over and do the breaking.

Horse breaking on the big cattle ranches in Texas was more than just taming a few mustangs. Each spring the rancher rounded up all of his horses, for most of them had been running free on the range all winter. The older ones which had become wild again had to be rebroken; the colts and the mustangs had to be broken for the first time.

On some of the larger ranches, horse breaking was a big job which needed a special crew. In some cases a group of cowboys worked from spring all through summer, doing nothing but breaking horses. These men frequently went from ranch to ranch "busting" for different owners.

The bronco busters were tough men who enjoyed the dangerous thrill of taming wild horses. Even the toughest of them lasted only a few years because this kind of riding ruined their kidneys and lungs. Some of them spit blood after a few months of busting. Because they were thrown so many times, they had their arms and legs broken over and over again.

There was far more to breaking a horse than just climbing on and trying to stay astride until it quit bucking. The wild horse was trained gradually. It first had to learn to respect a rope. It had to learn to stand quiet when a loop was thrown over its head. For if it ran to the end of the rope it would be thrown to the ground and choked. Yet each day for the first few days a wild horse ran as hard as it could, trying to break the thing it hated. When a bronco finally learned not to fight the rope, it was ready for its next lesson.

The cowboy then put a halter, called a "hackamore," on the partially subdued animal. The hackamore was a bitless bridle with which the cowboy could manage the horse without having the rope around its neck. The horse soon learned that if it pulled too hard the hackamore would tighten around its nose and cut off its breathing. The wild animal was then staked out to get used to the hackamore.

Finally the time came to break the horse to saddle. Cowboys roped and blindfolded it and held it while another cowboy threw a blanket and saddle on its back and tightened the cinches.

Then suddenly the bronc buster leaped into the saddle and snatched off the blindfold. The battle was on.

The horse's head went down and its hind legs went up. A bucking horse jumped high and came down stiff-legged, nearly jarring all the teeth out of the rider. The horse pitched and plunged, sometimes twisting in midair. If the cowboy stayed on its back, it might run full speed for a quarter of a mile, perhaps hoping that the rider would somehow disappear.

Even then a wild horse had a few tricks left. It could stop suddenly, trying to throw the rider over its head. It might rear so high that it nearly fell on its back. Sometimes it fell on its side and rolled, trying to crush the rider beneath it. But usually the cowboy was back in the saddle every time the horse got up.

Within a week the horse learned its lessons well. It knew that in trying to break a rope or hurt a cowboy it could hurt itself even more. Though it would make a few more efforts to gain its freedom, it was learning that its rider was its master. By the end of two or three weeks, it was ready to begin learning the skills of roundups and trail drives. Soon it would be a well-trained cow pony.

In Texas the rider on "the hurricane deck" of a bucking bronco was frequently a Negro cowboy. One named George was said to be the best bronc buster in Texas. Another was Joe McLeod who worked west of Nueces. When Joe found a really wild mustang he tamed it gradually, and then as one cowboy said, "That bronc likely became a one-man horse." One of the best was Bronco Sam, who was supposed to be able to ride any horse on the range. Cowboys used to say that a really wild horse acted as if it had a belly full of bedsprings, but that a good Negro horsebreaker could tame it.

There were lots of good horsebreakers in Texas, but there was also an outstanding Negro bronc buster up in Iowa who became a romantic figure in his neighborhood. For the small white boys of the community, he provided excitement and thrills. And to one of them he offered a chance to go West and become a cowboy.

The boy was Hubert Collins, the younger son of the local Methodist minister. His older brother had already gone to the cattle country, where he was a part owner of the Red Fork Ranch on the Cimarron River. Hubert kept bothering his parents to let him go West and join his brother, and they finally got tired of listening to him. They said that he could go if he was taken by an older man.

The man who agreed to take him was Jim Owsley, whom Hubert later remembered as a tall, handsome, broad-shouldered Negro. "Jim's business," Hubert wrote after he grew up, "was that of a horse trader, dealing in half-wild mustangs from the prairies of Texas. Each season he traveled by rail to Caldwell, Kansas, took the Chisholm Trail there and rode into the Lone Star State for his stock in trade. Driving them up the trail to Caldwell, he would ship them from there by rail into Corning. My playmates of those days must recall Jim and his herds. They combined to make excitement for us as they tore along our streets to the railroad cattle corrals, with a roar of hoof mingled with yells of men and squeals of frightened beasts, all hidden in a cloud of dust. I knew Jim, and had him enshrined as one of my heroes, and was therefore pleased when father asked him to take me on his next trip down the trail and leave me at Red Fork. He consented, and I lost no time in acquainting all my chums of my good fortune. I became a hero of the day within my circle."

Negro bronc busters were found even farther north than Iowa. Up in South Dakota there was one named Williams who broke horses to the saddle without breaking their spirits. Williams worked for a family named Lang, and the Lang family lived near Theodore Roosevelt, the man who later became President of the United States. So Theodore Roosevelt watched Williams break horses by winning their friendship and confidence. In a book which Lang wrote about ranching in the Bad Lands of the Dakotas, he said that Williams was a "past-master of the art—cool, collected, apparently fearless—if there was anything he did not know about handling horses, we never found it out. Moreover, if there was a horse in the range country that could throw him, nobody ever produced one." According to Lang's book, "Williams was the first to introduce sane horse breaking in our section of the country."

CHAPTER 11

Old Two Toes

✳❧ One Negro cowboy became well known to all his neighbors, but not for walking down mustangs or breaking wild horses. Willis Peoples was a cattleman who tracked down a killer wolf. How this Negro cowboy could do something that even professional wolf hunters could not do is told by Harry Chrisman in his book *Lost Trails of the Cimarron*.

Down "Crooked Creek to the Cimarron was a wild country infested with loafer wolves, 'catamounts,' coyotes, and other predators that gave cattlemen much trouble." All of these wild animals attacked the stock, but the big wolves were the most destructive because they could pull down and kill a full-grown cow and even severely cut up a range bull. A wolf known as "Old Two Toes" gave the cattlemen the most trouble. He got his name because he had once lost part of a front paw in a trap. The loss did not make him any less vicious, but made him easier to track.

The ranchers were determined to catch Old Two Toes,

whose trail of mangled cattle tripled when he mated with a large, black, and fierce she-wolf. The ranchers offered a reward for anyone who could hunt him down, and when no one succeeded, they raised the reward.

They brought in professional wolfers, hunters with experience and good reputation. The wolfers vainly followed the wolves from herd to herd, finding the bodies of cows and calves, but never surprising or even seeing Old Two Toes. They set baited traps and left poisoned meat. But the old wolf avoided the traps and scorned the meat. Finally the wolfers gave up.

One day Willis Peoples, who had a small ranch south of Meade, Kansas, near the Neutral Strip, came to town when the ranchers were talking about what they should do to keep Old Two Toes from destroying their cattle. Peoples offered them a proposition: if the ranchers would leave the wolves alone for one month and promise to help him in his campaign, he would guarantee to bring in the killer wolf. How, the cattlemen wanted to know, did Peoples think he could do this? He answered that he would camp on the trail of Old Two Toes day and night and would live with the wolf and its mate until the two wolves had their paws in the air while they begged forgiveness. Some of the ranchers in the town laughed, but those who knew Willis Peoples believed him.

Peoples got a Negro friend to keep him supplied with food, water, and fresh horses, the supplies to come from the ranch nearest to where he was each day. Then he got on his horse and headed for the scene of Old Two Toes' last kill.

Starting from there, he became a tracker, doggedly following the trail of the two wolves. Leaning from the saddle, his eyes always on the faint track of his prey, he began the long hunt. He went on day after day, stopping only when darkness hid the trail, and starting at the first light of dawn.

For two weeks he stayed on the trail, never quite overtaking the wolves, but never allowing them enough time to rest or hunt for food. Soon the she-wolf had enough and deserted her mate.

A few days later Peoples began to notice a weakening in the big wolf, and he realized that he was gaining an advantage. The trail was fresher and clearer and easier to read. The tired wolf was now less careful in hiding its tracks and doubling back.

Peoples became more watchful. When the tracks finally turned into a canyon and all the signs showed that the wolf was nearly crawling, Peoples rode more slowly.

Sure enough, he found it crouched ahead of him, sheltering under a high clay bank. He approached as close as he dared, and when the two were only fifty feet apart, he shot.

The next evening he drove into Meade and dropped Old Two Toes from his wagon into the street—a wolf which measured seven feet in length. The ranchers gathered to thank and to congratulate Willis Peoples. How, one asked, did he know from the outset that he could capture the wolf, especially when he knew that all the others, including the professional wolf hunters, had failed?

His answer was simple: the wolf represented "bad," at least it was "bad" for the community. Only "good" could kill the wolf. Willis Peoples was not sure that he was good enough, but he knew, he said, that any man with "his mind made up is a majority." His mind, he added, was made up, and that was "how it was."

Isom Dart and the Tip Gault Gang

✳︎ᚶᚩ   Isom Dart was born a slave on a hill farm in Arkansas. When the Civil War began, his master took him and several other slaves and moved farther south. Isom, who was just entering his teens, soon was serving a group of Confederate officers as orderly, cook, nurse, and scout— stealing fruit, chickens, or other food that could be used in the officers' mess.

When the war was over, Isom was free, but he had no job. So he began to drift down through Texas and into old Mexico. He worked at all kinds of jobs, and at one time he became a clown performing with a rodeo in Mexico. There he met a Mexican lad his own age named Terresa, and the two became partners in stealing horses south of the border. They swam the horses across the Rio Grande and sold them to Texas cattlemen.

Like all sensible horse thieves, Isom and Terresa soon

changed their place of operations. They moved north and west, eventually making their way into the northwest corner of Colorado, where the borders of Wyoming, Utah, and Colorado meet near the secluded valley of Brown's Hole. There they spent most of the rest of their lives.

For a time they separated, Terresa traveling with some local horse thieves and Isom trying life as a miner. That did not work out very well, so Isom worked for a while for a Chinese cook, and played poker after hours. But he soon had enough of cooking.

Having failed at mining and cooking, Isom turned to wild-horse hunting. Joining with a number of other men, he helped to construct a log corral at Charcoal Bottom on the Green River. Then he captured and broke wild horses. One author, John Rolfe Burroughs, wrote that "no man in the country understood horses better than Isom did." Another author, Dane Coolidge, wrote that Isom "was considered the best bronco rider that ever threw a leg over a horse." If Isom had stuck to wild horses, he might have led a longer and more peaceful life.

But he soon met Indians far wilder than any of his broncos. Into his camp rode a Shoshone Indian, a woman named Tickup, and her nine-year-old daughter Mincy. The mother was running from Pony Beater, her Indian husband. Pony Beater was cruel to both his wife and daughter. Tickup liked the big handsome Isom, and the two got along very well together.

For Isom this was a happy time. Not only did he get along with Tickup, but he found Mincy to be a charming little girl. Isom was the only decent father she had ever known, and the two adored each other.

Then Pony Beater appeared. He surprised Isom and whipped Tickup and Mincy. Tickup had had enough of her husband's brutality, so she took her daughter and returned to her own people in Idaho.

Isom went back to being a horse thief again. In the summer of 1875 he joined the Tip Gault gang of Brown's Hole. The gang was made up of Tip Gault, Jack Leath, Joe Pease, and Isom's old friend Terresa. It was a wild bunch who stole horses mostly for fun.

The fun, however, led to the death of all the gang except Isom. Their luck ran out when they spotted a big herd of horses being driven toward Wyoming cattle country. They scouted the herd for several days and decided to stampede and scatter it so that they could steal some of the horses without risking a head-on fight with the owner and his crew. When one of the horses spooked and ran out of the herd, they roped it and prepared to use it.

Their plan was simple: They would tie sagebrush to its tail and drive the frightened animal back toward the herd. With luck, the frantic horse would start a stampede. So while Terresa held a tight rein on the horse's head, Pease brought up the sagebrush. But just as he leaned out of the saddle, the horse kicked out with both feet and knocked him to the ground. He lay there unconscious, his jaw broken and his chest crushed.

Two of the gang took the injured man back toward their hidden camp while the other two chased the horse over the hill and into the travelling herd. All the animals stampeded and scattered, and soon the two thieves were rounding up many of them. As they did, they foolishly included in their roundup some of the horses of a local rancher.

Late that night the four thieves were reunited, and Isom learned that the badly wounded Pease had been unable to make it back to camp. He had been left under some trees about a half mile away. Isom agreed to act as nurse, for he had gained experience tending wounded men during the Civil War. He left the camp to watch over the dying Pease.

The next morning the gang found that the herd had moved on. Its owners had not tried to recover all their property. So Gault and his men searched the countryside for the rest of the scattered horses, not realizing that an angry local rancher was already tracking his missing saddle stock.

Isom stayed with Pease for a day and a night and most of another day before the patient died. Then Isom walked the half mile to camp, got a spade and returned to dig a grave. As he dug, the afternoon wore away and darkness came. His three friends rode back to camp, turned out their horses and began to make supper. They did not know that they had ridden into an ambush prepared by the rancher and a crew of heavily armed cowboys.

Still digging a grave, Isom heard the shots that killed his partners. Isom was unarmed, so he spent the long night crouching in the new grave he had dug.

The next morning he carefully made his way back to the campsite. He prepared a hasty breakfast, took everything that was left in the camp, and began walking.

Weeks later, after he had walked for miles, stolen a horse, and been wounded by its owner, Isom made his way to Green River City. There he decided to go straight, to make a fresh start. He wandered around the West for a time, but he became bored and missed his old days in

Brown's Hole. So he returned. There he signed on as a horse wrangler with the Middlesex Land and Cattle Company. He still had all his old skill with horses, and he still had his old love of adventure, whether inside or outside the law.

He became a devoted follower of Elizabeth Bassett, a stouthearted neighbor who had five children, a sick husband, and a small ranch. Along with a number of other cowboys, Isom Dart made her place a kind of second home. They soon came to be called the Bassett gang, partly because they never hesitated to "borrow" a steer if the ranch needed food.

As the years passed, their "borrowing" became rustling on a larger scale. The big neighboring Hoy and Scribner ranches began to lose more cattle than they could afford. They had suspicions, but they could not prove anything. The one time that they did get a Wyoming magistrate to issue a warrant for Isom, the Wyoming sheriff had a hard time finding a deputy to make an arrest. Finally he appointed the toughest of the local citizens, one Joe Philbrick, a deputy sheriff. He promised Philbrick a substantial reward if he would make the trip to Brown's Hole, arrest Isom Dart, and bring him in.

Philbrick made the trip in a buckboard. He found Isom and served the warrant without difficulty. Then he and his prisoner began the journey back to Wyoming, driving through rough country. Just as they reached the crest of a grade, a wheel slipped off the road, the horses started to bolt, and the buckboard fell down into a small canyon, taking the men and animals with it.

Although Philbrick was knocked unconscious, Isom was

unhurt. He could have escaped. But instead he tended the deputy's injuries, got the horses and buckboard back on the road, and drove on to Rock Springs, Wyoming. There he put Philbrick in the hospital and turned himself in at the jail.

His action was much praised by the community, and when he came to trial the deputy appeared in his favor. After Philbrick had finished telling what Isom had done, the jury ignored the fact that Isom was being tried for cattle stealing. The jury decided that anyone who helped another the way Isom had done was no menace to society, so they turned him loose. Isom went back to Brown's Hole.

Among the best of his friends were a number of children. After Mrs. Bassett's daughter married Jim McKnight and had two boys, Isom spent much of his time amusing and taking care of them. He sang them old songs he remembered from his youth on a slave plantation. Sometimes he put on little shows for them, as he used to do when he was a clown with the Mexican rodeo. Little Chick McKnight once said to his mother, "Mama, I'll never have to go to a circus, 'cause I got a circus all my own."

Isom settled down and returned to his old work of catching and breaking wild horses. According to an author, Dean Krakel, Isom was "one of the best cowboys ever to mount a horse in the high mesa country." One man from Brown's Hole, who said he had seen all the great riders, thought that Isom was the greatest of them all.

With all this skill, Isom slowly built up a ranch of his own. He did it mostly by catching wild horses, breaking them, and then trading them for cattle.

One of his friends was Matt Rash, a cattleman from

Texas. They both became successful in the cattle business, and they both died at the hands of the same man.

Their killer was Tom Horn, long famous in the West as a range detective, Indian fighter, "regulator," and murderer. Hired by one or more Wyoming cattlemen, Horn rode down into Brown's Hole looking for rustlers. Although he was a killer, Tom Horn was a good cowboy and a friendly man. He found it easy to win the trust of the men he was trying to catch.

He seems even to have liked the men he was after, because he sent them notes trying to scare them away. But Matt Rash and Isom Dart would not leave. Rash had built a large ranch and planned to marry a local girl. Dart, at age fifty, decided he was too old to leave his ranch and his friends.

Matt Rash died first. Tom Horn crept up to his door and shot him as he ate breakfast.

Now Isom Dart was frightened, but he was stubborn. He stayed on his ranch, but he kept a number of friends around. Friends, however, could not protect him from a sharpshooter with a new 30-30 Winchester rifle. About three months after the murder of Rash, Isom Dart was shot and killed as he walked out of his cabin with two of his friends. While the friends dropped and crawled for cover, the killer escaped unseen.

Isom Dart was buried in a shallow grave on Cold Spring Mountain. He was mourned by his good friends and by at least two young boys who had lost a companion, a playmate, and a circus.

CHAPTER 13

Cherokee Bill—the Worst One of All

✳️⊰   There is a famous picture of Billy the Kid which shows a shabby, pop-eyed, buck-toothed young man staring vacantly into the camera lens. Yet Billy has become the best known of all the Western badmen, the subject of many books, the hero of stories, ballads, and even a ballet. The slow growth of legend has made a kind of American Robin Hood out of a tough, ugly kid.

Another man who was really handsome, though just as tough and twice as vicious as Billy, was the cowboy who rode into the Red Fork Ranch in the Indian Territory (Oklahoma) about ten years after Billy's death. He was tall and graceful, a copper-skinned man whose long, wavy black hair fell to his shoulders. His clothing and Stetson were expensive, his bridle silver mounted, and his rope made of black and white horse hair. He was cheerful and charming and gracious.

The young ranch owner thought, quite correctly, that his guest was part Indian, part Negro, but welcomed him willingly. "No matter what his parentage," wrote an observer, "Red Fork Ranch was entertaining a young man who was as full of life and the joy of living as ever passed that way. His life's history (his own version), stories and anecdotes came in a constant flow. He sang ditties, danced jigs and indulged in good-natured banter at the expense of the ranchman, to while away the afternoon and evening."

Next morning the lively guest made preparations for a trip to the Panhandle. He put on a heavy coat and buckskin gloves, buckled on his gun belt, and stowed his Winchester in its saddle holster. Then he leaped onto his horse.

"For two or three minutes he reined in the beast with one hand and allowed it to buck-jump from pure fullness of spirits. With every jump of the animal, the man let out a whoop of the same joy that animated the bronco. Then giving the horse the rein with a final yell, he tore away, turning in the saddle to doff his hat in graceful adieu, and waving it to and fro till he had passed from sight."

The charming guest was Cherokee Bill, an outlaw who fascinated women, murdered countless men for fun and profit, and died on the gallows only a month after his twentieth birthday. He was born at Fort Concho, Texas, in 1876, of parents who were part Negro, part white, and part Indian.

Bill began his short career at the age of fourteen when he shot and killed his brother-in-law. After that, he became a professional killer, shooting railroad agents, Indian police, express agents, and storekeepers. He rode with a gang specializing in the armed robbery of stores, trains, and express offices. He killed casually and gleefully, and inspired fear and horror throughout the Indian Territory. According to Glenn Shirley, an author who wrote about this badman, Cherokee Bill made desperadoes like John Wesley Hardin and Sam Bass look like "small potatoes" at a time when "there was no Sunday west of St. Louis, and no God west of Fort Smith."

For women he seems to have had irresistible charm. He was said to have "a sweetheart in nearly every section of the country," and for several years he traveled freely through the Indian Territory without being challenged. To protect itself, at least one town passed a law which said that nobody could bother him while he was in its limits. So Cherokee Bill could mount his bronco and ride gaily from crime to crime and from woman to woman.

His very success led to his downfall. As his crimes increased, the reward money posted for his capture also mounted. With his successes he became careless. Once while he was visiting his favorite sweetheart, Maggie Glass, he relaxed too much. When he was not looking he was hit on the head with a poker swung by Ike Rogers, Maggie's cousin.

Handcuffed and chained, Bill was turned over to deputy United States marshals and carried to Fort Smith, Arkansas. There he was tried before Judge Parker, a man widely known for quick trials and severe sentences. Though Cherokee Bill had been accused of many crimes, he was tried and convicted for the murder of one unarmed man in a post-office robbery. Later he was convicted of a second murder, the killing of a prison jailer.

When Judge Parker sentenced him to hang, the judge said that he was sorry there was no harsher penalty.

"Your record," the judge said, "is more atrocious than that of all the criminals who have hitherto stood before this bar. To effect your capture brave men risked their lives and it was only by the keenest strategy that it was effected. Even after you had been placed within the prison walls your ferocity prevented docility, and your only thought was to break away that you might return to the scenes of bloodshed from which an outraged law had estranged you. In order to make your escape you would have trampled under foot the will of the people, and releasing hundreds of your ilk, fled to your mountain and forest haunts, there to gather around you a larger and more bloodthirsty band; there to defy all power under heaven while you indulged your passion for crime; there to burn and pillage and destroy the lives of whoever stood for a moment in the way of your campaign of destruction. . . ."

The judge had even more to say, for he always liked to talk. But not Cherokee Bill, who finally walked to his public execution. When he was asked if he had anything to say to the crowd, he answered, "No. I came here to die—not to make a speech."

CHAPTER 14

Deadwood Dick

$500 Reward: For the apprehension and arrest of a notorious young desperado who hails to the name of Deadwood Dick. His present whereabouts are somewhat contiguous to the Black Hills. For further information, and so forth apply immediately to

HUGH VANSEVERE
At Metropolitan Saloon, Deadwood City

Thus read a notice posted up against a big pine tree, three miles above Custer City, on the banks of French Creek. It was a large placard tacked up in plain view of all passers-by, who took the route north through Custer gulch in order to reach the infant city of the Northwest—Deadwood.

A horseman rode by and noticed the placard so prominently posted for public inspection. With a low whistle, expressive of astonishment, he wheeled his horse out of the stage road, and rode over to the foot of the tree in question and ran his eyes over the few irregularly-written lines traced upon the notice.

He was a youth of an age somewhere between sixteen and

twenty, trim and compactly built, with a preponderance of muscular development and animal spirits; broad and deep of chest, with square, iron-cast shoulders; limbs small yet like bars of steel, and with a grace of position in the saddle rarely equaled; he made a fine picture for an artist's brush or a poet's pen.

Only one thing marred the captivating beauty of the picture.

His form was clothed in a tight-fitting habit of buckskin, which was colored a jetty black, and presented a striking contrast to anything one sees as a garment in the wild far West. And this was not all, either. A broad black hat was slouched down over his eyes; he wore a thick black mask over the upper portion of his face, through the eyeholes of which there gleamed a pair of orbs of piercing intensity, and his hands, large and knotted, were hidden in a pair of kid gloves.

The "Black Rider" he might have been justly termed, for his thoroughbred steed was as black as coal, but we have not seen fit to call him such—his name is Deadwood Dick, and let that suffice for the present.

So began the first of a famous series of dime novels, a wild tale of adventure printed on cheap paper and published in 1877. It was called *Deadwood Dick, The Prince of the Road; or, The Black Rider of the Black Hills*. It was read by thousands of boys, as were more than a hundred other later novels about Deadwood Dick and Deadwood Dick, Jr.

But there never was a real Deadwood Dick like the hero of the novels. There was only the name—a name that many real men claimed at one time or another.

One of these men was a Negro cowboy. Perhaps because he remembered that the dime novel hero had been the "Black Rider of the Black Hills," he claimed to be the original Deadwood Dick. So when he wrote a book about the story of his life, he called it *The Life and Adventures of Nat Love: Better Known in the Cattle Country as "Deadwood Dick"—By Himself.*

Many of the cowboys and cattlemen of the West who wrote books about themselves stretched the truth at times. They told stories that people knew were a little "tall." Nat Love, in his book, was like these other writers. When you read the story of his life, you know that some of it cannot be true. Yet it is a good story which tells us much about the West and about the part that one Negro cowboy may have played in its development.

Nat Love was born in an old log cabin in Tennessee, about seven years before the Civil War began. He never knew the day of his birth because in those days people generally did not keep records of the births of slave babies. His parents were owned by Robert Love: his father was a foreman of the slaves, and his mother had charge of the kitchen at the big house. He grew up with almost no education, because white owners rarely bothered to send slave children to school.

When the Civil War was over Nat's family were set free, but they had a hard time because they had no money. Then Nat's father died. This made young Nat, at the age of about twelve, the head of the household. Only after three or four years of the hardest kind of struggles were they finally able to take care of themselves, and then the young man could go out into the world on his own.

Before he left home Nat got a job which helped prepare him for cowboy life. A neighbor, Mr. Williams, owned a horse ranch on which there were a number of young colts. He hired Nat to break the colts for ten cents apiece. For a time Nat made money while he had fun. Then one day he was asked to break a big, wild stallion. For this job he got twenty-five cents—paid in advance. He finally broke the big horse, but only after a wild ride which took him through several pastures, stampeded a number of horses, and stirred up all the dogs in the neighborhood. Then he discovered, at the end of the ride, that he had lost his quarter. It had been shaken out of his pocket.

Nat's chance to see more of the world came when he won a horse in a raffle. He sold the horse and gave half of the money to his mother. Then he went out West.

When Nat Love left home at the age of fifteen he had heard about the cattle drives from southern Texas into Kansas. So the young horsebreaker headed for "trail's end" in the cattle country. Arriving in a typical frontier town, he saw saloons, dance halls, gambling houses, cowboys and "very little of anything else." Seeing the cowboys on their prancing horses, Nat decided to share their life.

The next morning he found a Texas outfit that had delivered its herd and was preparing to go back down the trail to Texas. There were several good Negro cowboys in the outfit. After sharing breakfast with the crew, Nat asked the trail boss for a job. The boss agreed, if the young man could break Good Eye, the wildest horse in the outfit. Bronco Jim, a Negro cowboy, gave Nat some pointers, and Nat wore down the horse, although he later admitted that it was the toughest ride he had ever made. Having won his job, he rode down the trail to Texas to begin life as a cowboy.

During his first few months with a cattle outfit, Nat learned that the work was the hardest he had ever done in his life. He rode through hailstorms so violent that only strong men could stand them. When he first met hostile Indians, he admitted, he was too badly scared to run. But after going through a number of such trials he had so adjusted himself to the ways of the cattle country that he could handle any problem, especially because he was born with "a genuine love of the free and wild life of the range." Soon, he said, he was known as a good all-round cowboy.

Nat's home ranch was on the Palo Duro River in the Texas Panhandle. There he worked for three years, taking part in all the activities of the range, including the drives to Kansas cattle towns. He was happy with the companionship he had with other cowboys, and he thought that all men were pretty much the same when they had the earth for a bed and the sky for covering.

As a boy in Tennessee, Nat had hunted rabbits. In Texas he learned that guns were sometimes used to shoot at men. So he took every opportunity to practice with his forty-five. There came a day when he could shoot better than his friends.

When Nat left the Texas Panhandle, he rode into Arizona, where he worked for an outfit on the Gila River. By this time he had ridden many of the trails of the Southwest, and he believed that he had become a capable cowboy. In Arizona he learned two more things. While working with Mexican vaqueros he learned, he said, to speak Spanish like a native. More important for his boss, he became very good at reading brands. He soon was the chief brand reader for his outfit.

Sometimes, Nat wrote, the cattlemen got into violent arguments over brands. In some of these arguments the

cowboys shot each other. Law in Arizona at that time depended on who had the most courage and the fastest gun.
In Holbrook, Arizona, Nat saw an affair which began
among his friends when they quarreled over the ownership
of a horse. It was a sad thing, he said, to see three of his
friends dead and others wounded.

In his book Nat Love told about many of the things
which happened to him while he was a cowboy on the
plains.

He was in many stampedes during his days of driving
longhorns up the trail, but one of the most exciting was a
buffalo stampede. He and his outfit were driving longhorns
up the Western Trail to Nebraska one summer when suddenly they heard a roar like thunder. Although they could
hear it before they saw anything, they could tell from the
loud noise that it was a buffalo stampede. And when the
sound became louder and louder, they knew the stampeding buffalo were headed for them and their cattle.

The cowboys immediately tried to get their longhorns
to move faster, hoping to get them out of the way of the on-
coming buffalo. But no matter what they did, they could
not head the buffalo off. So the cowboys rode out to meet
the approaching stampede. As they rode they began to
shoot the buffalo. They hoped that if they killed enough
of those in front that those in back would change course.
Nothing worked.

Nat said that the buffalo "paid no more attention to us
than they would have paid to a lot of boys with pea shoot-
ers." The great maddened, plunging, snorting herd kept
coming. Finally the buffalo ran right over and through the
herd of cattle. Five of the steers were left dead, and many

were injured. Longhorns were scattered all over the plain.

Worst of all, one of the cowboys was also killed. He could not control his horse when it became frightened. It bolted and fell right in front of the buffalo herd. The cowboy just disappeared. The other cowboys could find only a few scraps of his clothing. Even his horse had been stamped on by so many buffalo that according to Nat it had been reduced to the size of a jack rabbit.

Nat told many stories about fighting Indians. One of his battles occurred on the way back to Arizona from Dodge City, where he and his outfit had delivered a large herd of horses. The cowboys, according to Nat, were surprised by a band of Indians. The Indians, on horseback, rode full speed at the smaller group of cowboys, firing as they rode. For a few minutes the cowboys fought back. Then they realized that there were far too many Indians, so they turned and began to ride for their lives. Nat Love's horse was shot from under him, and at the same time Nat's partner, James Holley, was shot and killed. Nat was lucky enough to catch the animal of the dead cowboy and ride it to safety.

Nat enjoyed an occasional fight. Once when he had gone down to Old Mexico after some horses, he decided to stir up some trouble. He was irritable and thirsty, and so he turned toward a local saloon. He rode his horse right through the swinging doors, firing his gun as he rode. He stopped his horse at the bar and ordered a drink.

Soon the Mexicans had recovered from their first fear and astonishment. When they started to reach for their own weapons, Nat spurred his horse and rode back out, but he was almost too slow. The Mexicans opened fire and wounded Nat's horse, though they missed its rider.

This kind of dangerous foolishness sometimes came from too much liquor. Once, for instance, Nat found himself idle in Dodge City at the end of a long cattle drive. For a while he and his friends tried to drink all the bad whiskey in town. They did not succeed, but Nat drank enough to become both thoughtless and restless.

Later that night, riding back to camp, Nat passed old Fort Dodge, about five miles from Dodge City. And there he saw a cannon. At that moment, he said, "a bright idea struck me, but a fool one just the same." He decided to rope the cannon and take it back to Texas to fight Indians with.

Uncoiling his lariat, Nat rode for the cannon, ignoring the guard's orders to halt. He roped the cannon, all right, but it would not budge. In the meantime the sentry at the gate blew his bugle to give the alarm, and several soldiers ran to mount their horses. Nat decided that he had made a foolish mistake, and so he wheeled his horse and rode out through the gate onto the open prairie.

The soldiers mounted and went after him at full gallop. He spurred his horse, but the tired cattle pony was no match for fresh cavalry horses. The soldiers soon caught Nat and put him under arrest.

Once lodged in the guardhouse, Nat had time to regret both his bad whiskey and his bright idea. Now that he was nearly sober and looking out at the world through bars, he had no desire to drag an Army cannon back to Texas on the end of a lariat. He just wanted to get out of jail.

Fortunately for Nat, the fort's commanding officer thought the whole incident was a great joke. He laughed and ordered the cowboy's release. Nat rode back to Texas without trying any more drunken pranks.

In the spring of 1876, Nat Love's outfit received an order for three thousand three-year-old steers to be delivered at Deadwood in the Dakota Territory. According to Nat's account, the cowboys arrived near Deadwood on July 3 and delivered the herd. Then they got ready for the Fourth. Deadwood, on July 4, 1876, was a brand new town. The famous Homestakes gold mine had recently been discovered. This made Deadwood a boom town, full of miners, cowboys, and gamblers.

The town was ready for the cowboys when they rode in on the morning of the Fourth. The mining men and gamblers had got together and organized a contest. For this they had collected two hundred dollars for prize money. Six of the dozen men in the contest, Nat reported, were Negroes. Each cowboy was to rope, throw, tie, bridle, and saddle a mustang in the shortest possible time. The horses were chosen for wildness, not for gentleness. Nat told what happened: "I roped, threw, tied, bridled, saddled, and mounted my mustang in exactly nine minutes from the crack of the gun. The time of the next competitor was twelve minutes and thirty seconds. This gave me the record and the championship of the West, which I held up to the time I quit the business."

With the roping contest done, an argument arose over who was the best shot. So a shooting contest was arranged for the afternoon. A range was measured off for the rifle contest at 100 and 250 yards. The range for the Colts was set at 150 yards. Each cowboy had fourteen shots with the rifle and twelve shots with his Colt. Nat placed all of his rifle shots in the bull's eye and ten of his twelve pistol shots in the center! His nearest competitor hit only eight with the rifle and five with the forty-five.

The winner and "hero of Deadwood" was Nat Love, the Negro cowboy and former slave. Along with the prize money, the grateful and excited men of Deadwood gave Nat the title of "Deadwood Dick," a name which he carried with "honor" ever after.

Although much of Nat Love's book sounds like a typical tall story of the Wild West, many of the things that he told about did happen. Many cowboys fought Indians, rode wild horses, and did some fancy shooting. Bose Ikard, for instance, rode through hostile Indian country, carrying thousands of dollars in gold and trading shots with outlaws. Both white and Negro cowboys won riding, roping, and shooting contests. So Nat's story about his own life is much the same as those stories told by other cowboys about their adventures on the plains.

When Nat Love published his book in 1907, he let his "chest swell with pride" because he was an American. He expressed his feelings this way: "Such was life on the western ranges when I rode them, and such were my comrades and surroundings; humor and tragedy. In the midst of life we were in death, but above all showed the universal manhood. The wild and free life. The boundless plains. The countless thousands of longhorn steers, the wild fleet-footed mustangs. The buffalo and other game, the delight of living, and the fights against death that caused every nerve to tingle, and every day communion with men, whose minds were as broad as the plains they roamed, and whose creed was every man for himself and every friend for each other, and with each other till the end."

CHAPTER 15

The Wonderful Bill Pickett

✳✿ In the old days on the plains when the cowboys went out to break horses it was hard work. It was some years later that they did it just for fun and excitement. That was when the rodeos began.

The same thing happened in bulldogging.

From the earliest days of trail driving it was sometimes necessary to rope steers which broke away from the herd. Roping a running steer was not easy. The cowboy often threw many misses, and the steer could be a long way from the herd before it was brought down. At times a cowboy forgot his rope and then he tried to bring down a steer by hand.

The most common method was for the cowboy to ride alongside the steer, reach down and grab it by the horns, leave his horse and get his feet out in front. Then by digging his heels into the ground he could slow down the steer. At the same time he began to twist the animal's head and neck. If all went well the cowboy could finally stop the steer and throw it.

Philip Ashton Rollins, one of the men who described life on the plains, wrote about bulldogging this way: "Bulldogging involved throwing one's right arm over a steer's or cow's neck, the right hand gripping the neck's loose bottom skin or the base of the right horn or the brute's nose, while the left hand seized the tip of the brute's left horn. The 'dogger' then rose clear of the ground; and, by lunging his body downward against his own left elbow, so twisted the neck of the brute that the latter lost its balance and fell. It was a somewhat active performance, because the instant the dogger took hold, the seized beast began to run, and the man's legs, when not touching the ground in flying leaps, were waving outward to avoid his maddened vehicle's knees."

Usually a cowboy could get more done and do it easier with a rope. So bulldogging was a last resort. But it happened.

About ten years after the end of the Civil War, for instance, a cattleman named Bill Hudson bought a large herd of longhorns and spent a long day bunching them together for a drive to Kansas. Then he and his men gathered around the chuck wagon for supper.

Suddenly a steer broke out of the herd and could not be driven back. Many cowboys mounted their horses and attempted to turn or rope the animal, but they were unsuccessful.

Then a Negro cowboy named Andy, a man who was one of Hudson's top riders and ropers, looked for his own lariat. When he could not find it, he jumped on his horse and chased off empty handed. Riding up to the steer, he reached down and caught its nose in one hand and a horn in another. He twisted the steer's nose up and threw him, jumping from the saddle as he did so.

Harry Chrisman wrote about another Negro cowboy, Sam Johnson, who bulldogged a Texas longhorn with horns spreading six feet from tip to tip. Those who saw Johnson's performance thought they had seen one of the best cowboy shows in Kansas.

When cowboys began to put on shows and eventually rodeos in towns in Texas, Colorado, and Wyoming, bulldogging became popular. And at the rodeos the man who was thought to be just about the best bulldogger in the country was the Negro cowboy Bill Pickett. According to Pickett's boss, Zack Miller, "Bill Pickett was the greatest sweat-and-dirt cowhand that ever lived—bar none."

Many authors have described the wonderful feats of Bill Pickett, but the one who told the most complete story of Pickett's life was Fred Gipson in *Fabulous Empire*. His book dealt with the Miller brothers and their fabulous 101 Ranch.

When Bill Pickett joined the 101 Ranch in the Strip in Oklahoma at the end of the last century, it was a big outfit. The Miller brothers' ranch covered more than 100,000 acres and employed 200 men.

The 101 became known for having some of the best cowhands on the range. Kurt Reynolds was the all-round cowboy; Johnny Brewer could ride anything that bucked; Jim Hopkins could lay his rope over any steer's horns; Bill Pickett and Lon Sealy were unmatched as bulldoggers; George Hooker, another Negro, was a trick rider who could do almost anything.

Then the Miller brothers hired Tom Mix, who was said to be a better bartender than horseman. But Mix looked the part of a cowboy and he learned quickly. He later became a famous movie star.

Will Rogers was not a regular 101 hand, but for several years, at intervals, he put up with and worked with the 101 cowboys. Rogers specialized in rope tricks, and most people thought that he could do more with a rope than anyone else in the country. He later became famous both on Broadway in New York and in the movies in Hollywood.

Bill Pickett was no ordinary bulldogger. In 1900, around the time he joined the 101 Ranch, he was a man about forty years old, "a big-handed, wild-riding South Texas brush-popper" with a style of bulldogging so startling and so different that many thought that he had invented the sport. Today if you go to a rodeo in a little town in the West you may see on the program a note that Bill Pickett invented bulldogging.

Bill Pickett's style went beyond that of any other cowboy. According to Fred Gipson, "The way Bill went at it, he piled out of his saddle onto the head of a running steer, sometimes jumping five or six feet to tie on. He'd grab a horn in each hand and twist them till the steer's nose came up. Then he'd reach in and grab the steer's upper lip with his strong white teeth, throw up his hands to show he wasn't holding any more, and fall to one side of the steer, dragging along beside him till the animal went down."

This was bulldogging the way the bulldogs did it, taking "guts, bull strength, and the same peculiar sense of timing that makes art out of dancing."

Bill Pickett was in his prime in the summer of 1904 when the citizens of Cheyenne, Wyoming, put on their famous

"Frontier Day" celebration. Visitors came from all around the country. Cowboys came from the various cattle ranches. Shoshone Indians came from their reservation. Thousands of people walked the streets of Cheyenne, tooting horns, yelling, and throwing confetti. Everyone was in a gay mood for the celebration. Early in the afternoon, 20,000 people went out to the arena to see the famous rodeo.

The Frontier Day celebration was so important that *Harper's Weekly* in New York sent a man out to Wyoming just to write about the event. The writer watched the steer roping, bronc busting, and maverick branding with great excitement. But when he saw Bill Pickett do his bull-dogging act, the New Yorker thought that it was the most remarkable event of the whole celebration.

Pickett, he wrote, "gave his exhibition while 20,000 people watched with wonder and admiration—a mere unarmed man who attacked a fiery, wild-eyed, and powerful steer and threw it by his teeth.

"With the aid of a helper, Pickett chased the steer until it was in front of the grandstand. Then he jumped from the saddle and landed on the back of the animal, grasped its horns, and brought it to a stop within a dozen feet. By a remarkable display of strength he twisted the steer's head until its nose pointed straight into the air.

"Again and again the Negro was jerked from his feet and tossed into the air, but his grip on the horns never once loosened, and the steer failed in its efforts to gore him. Suddenly Pickett dropped the steer's head and grasped the upper lip of the animal with his teeth, and threw his arms wide apart, to show that he was not using his hands."

The New York writer finished his piece by adding that the "crowd was speechless."

The 101 Ranch put on its first big rodeo for the 1905 convention of the National Editors' Association. The editors, meeting in Guthrie, Oklahoma, went up to the ranch on the Salt Fork for the show. Thirty-five special trains could not carry the crowd. It was a great show, and the newspapermen gave it lots of publicity.

For the next several years the Miller Brothers 101 Ranch became famous for putting on one of the finest rodeos in the world, and it played in such places as Chicago, New York, London, and Mexico City. One of the programs listed the following events:

1:30 P.M.   GRAND PARADE

Indians, Cowboys, Prairie Schooners, Ox Wagons, Oklahoma Farmers, Modern Farm Machinery, Steam Plow, Automobiles, 12 Bands

2:15 P.M.   BUFFALO CHASE

2:30 P.M.   INDIAN SPORTS AND DANCES

2:50 P.M.   MISS LUCILE MULHALL AND HER HORSE, "GOVERNOR"

MR. GEO. ELSER, Champion Trick Rider of the World

3:20 P.M.   RIDING WILD BRONCOS

4:00 P.M.   CHAMPION STEER ROPING CONTEST

4:45 P.M.   THE WONDERFUL NEGRO "PICKETT"

Throwing Wild Steer by the Nose with His Teeth

5:00 P.M.   COWBOYS AND GIRLS IN HORSEBACK QUADRILLE

5:15 P.M.   BURNING EMIGRANT WAGON TRAIN BY INDIANS

5:30 P.M.   RECEPTION BY THE INDIANS

"Home, Sweet Home"

For several years the 101 hands put on shows for people all over the United States. One of the best times they had was in New York, where they played in Madison Square Garden.

The kind of horse show that the Garden had been putting on had been unprofitable, and the management was looking for something more exciting. When Zack Miller was asked how much it would cost to bring his outfit to New York, he decided to go for the fun, the publicity, and his expenses. His cowhands had a good time and expenses ran a little high, but New Yorkers were treated to some amazing feats of riding, roping, and bull-dogging.

The first night in Madison Square Garden the cowboys performed for a small crowd, but only the first night. Bill Pickett's act was featured, but the steer was unruly. Frightened by the crowd and angered by the noise, the steer came out of the chute so fast it got the jump on Pickett's horse. Before Pickett could catch the steer it had crossed the arena and jumped a gate. It knocked off the top boards, and landed in the grandstand. The people screamed and scattered.

Pickett, on his horse, also jumped the gate and rode right after the steer. Will Rogers was in the act—to do the hazing for Pickett—so he too followed. Amid the scrambling, screaming customers, Pickett rode the steer down and bulldogged it. By this time Rogers had also ridden into the stands and with his spinning rope picked up the steer's heels. With Pitckett hanging on the steer's horns, Rogers dragged the animal back down the stairs into the arena.

The newspaper coverage, that first night, was enough to pack the Garden for the rest of the performances. There was no more bulldogging in the stands, but Bill Pickett brought down steers with his teeth, Will Rogers amazed the crowd with his rope tricks, and Tom Mix thrilled the ladies with his dashing riding.

One time the Miller brothers decided to take the show to Mexico City. There they found that the Mexicans were very fond of bullfighting, but they did not think much of an American rodeo.

The cowboys did not know much about bullfighting, and they had no idea how important it was to the Mexicans. So they made the Mexicans angry when they claimed that "Bill Pickett's bulldogging act was a greater show than any Mexican bullfight." Then one of the Miller brothers said that Bill Pickett could throw two steers in the time it would take two Mexican bullfighters to throw one.

Finally the cowboys bet the bullfighters that Pickett could hold on to one of the fighting bulls for five minutes. The contest was billed as part of the rodeo.

When the day arrived the stands were packed, but not with rodeo fans or friends. The opening acts were booed, for the audience had come to see only one thing—the death of a Negro cowboy who dared to wrestle a fighting bull with his bare hands.

From the beginning Pickett had a lot of trouble because, although his horse was expert at chasing steers, it could not work in close enough to the bull. Eventually, and only after the bull had gored his horse's rump, Bill slid off over the horse's tail and grabbed the bull's horns. "For the next two minutes," according to Fred Gipson's account, "the bull made a whipcracker out of Bill Pickett. He slammed the Negro's body against the arena wall. He threw up his head to sling the clinging man creature right and left, trying to dislodge him. He whipped him against another wall. He reached with his forefeet and tried to paw him loose. Finally he got down on his knees and drove his sharp horns into the ground, time and again, trying to run Bill through."

Gradually Pickett began to wear down the bull's strength, but then the customers began to throw a variety of things at the bull-dogger. When he was hit in the ribs with a beer bottle, he loosened his hold, and thereafter he could only hang on while the bull threw him about in violent fashion. After six minutes it became clear that the timer did not intend to ring the bell at all. So the 101 hands rode into the ring and roped the bull. The crowd went wild and threw everything it could get hold of, but the cowboys won the bet from the bullfighters.

Bill Pickett lived for many years. In the spring of 1914 the 101 Ranch was invited to take part in the Anglo-American Exposition to be held in London. One of the Miller brothers took half of the New York show, including Pickett and George Hooker, the Negro trick rider, and shipped for England.

The Miller brothers' rodeo performed successfully in London for several months. A special show was arranged for England's royalty, and Pickett put on his bulldogging act for King George V and Queen Mary. After Bill shook hands with the King and Queen, he went to dinner with an English earl.

The success of the Miller brothers' show in London came to an abrupt end on August 7, 1914. World War I had come to England. Under a national emergency order the government took over all of the Miller brothers' horses and vehicles except six horses and a wagon. The show was over: it was time to go home.

It was many years before the Miller brothers could put their show together again, and when they did it was never as good as the one they had in those years before the war.

By 1932 only one of the Miller brothers was still alive. The once-famous 101 Ranch had gradually dwindled away.

In 1932, Zack, the remaining Miller brother, became ill, and Bill Pickett, the only one of the old 101 riders still with him, was his companion and nurse. To please the ailing Miller, Pickett, then in his seventies, went to the corral to cut out some horses. When roped, one big sorrel gave Bill trouble by rearing and plunging. Bill was an old man now, and he was not as fast as he had been. He tried to duck out of the way, but he was too slow. One of the horse's hooves caught him on the head and knocked him down. The sorrel then stomped and kicked him.

Eleven days later Bill Pickett was dead. Zack Miller arranged his burial, placing his grave high on a hill. His grave was dug deep, well protected from the coyotes who still prowled over the surrounding range land.

On the day Bill Pickett died, his old boss wrote a poem in Bill's honor. It went like this:

> Old Bill has died and gone away, over the "Great
> Divide."
> Gone to a place where the preachers say both saint
> and sinner will abide.
> If they "check his brand" like I think they will
> it's a runnin' hoss
> They'll give to Bill

And some good wild steers till he gets his fill.
And a great big crowd for him to thrill.

Apparently the cowhand did have the showmanship and ability to thrill a crowd. According to Fred Gipson, Bill Pickett at his best was really something to watch. "When old Bill Pickett tied onto a runaway steer's nose with his teeth and busted him against the ground, the crowd reared up on its hind legs screaming. Right down to the last puff of dust kicked up in the arena, that show was wilder than a wolf."

The Peerless Jesse Stahl

✳ᘓᗝ While the Wonderful Bill Pickett was thrilling crowds around the world, other Negro cowboys were putting on a spine-tingling show in California. One of them came to be called the best bronc rider in the world. He was known as the Peerless Jesse Stahl.

It all began in 1911, when the little town of Salinas, California, decided to carry on the traditions of the old West. There were still many ranches in the beautiful Salinas Valley that drifts down between the rugged Big Sur Mountains and the Gabilan mountain range. Mountain lions still prowled in the foothills, and blooded cattle grazed in the valleys. But the old way of life was already changing as farmers planted more and more acres with lettuce and other crops.

So the citizens of Salinas decided to celebrate the old days with a "Big Week" of rodeo. They planned and carried it through so successfully that their big week became an annual event, an established tradition. Today this California Rodeo has become one of the "Big Four" of the world, a contest that draws the very best competitors from all over America.

Even the very first rodeo had plenty of cowboys to ride bucking broncs and to bulldog steers. But it also had other attractions, because many of the things that are common today were new to the people of that time.

The Wright brothers had invented the airplane only a few years before. Not all the people in the country had seen one in 1911. But those who went to the Salinas Rodeo could see a real "flying machine." They could also see a "balloon ascension," which some people found more exciting than bronc busting.

Another attraction brought hundreds of people by train from San Francisco. Barney Oldfield, the country's famous racing driver, was in Salinas to put on a show with his "freak machine." Even a racing car was a new and exciting sideshow in those days.

But horses and cattle were the main attraction. Cowboys competed in "chariot races," and they gave exciting bull-dogging and bronc-busting performances. They helped to advertise the rodeo by proclaiming that the broncs were "absolutely loco"—outlaw horses that could buck all night. And the broncs put on such a show that the rodeo became famous.

By July of 1916, when the California Rodeo "opened with a whoop," members of the Humane Society became suspicious. They came down from San Francisco to inspect the affair because they had heard that someone was putting tacks under the saddles to make the horses buck. The sheriff met them and showed them around. He assured them that they were mistaken. The broncs did not need any tacks, he said. They were already wild enough.

So were the cowboys, whose exploits were breathlessly reported every year by the Salinas *Californian* (in those days called the Salinas *Daily Index*). Their performances —in and out of the arena—made headlines during each big rodeo week. Only in 1915, when the rodeo people agreed not to compete for crowds with the Panama-Pacific Exposition going on in San Francisco, did cowboys fail to make the summer an exciting one. That year the Salinas citizens had to go to the White Theater to get their thrills from flickering silent movies like *Arizona* and *Outlaw's Reform*.

Almost from the very beginning, Negro cowboys took part in the show. The California Rodeo of 1916, for instance, included Jesse Stahl, Ambrose Stahl, Ty Stokes, W. J. Cole, and Frank Greenway, all of whom were Negroes.

Ty Stokes, headlined as a Fancy Trick Rider, was "heartily cheered." According to the newspaper, he "excelled." Ty Stokes "varied his program by riding standing on his neck with his feet straight above the saddle. His leaping from the galloping horse to the ground and then vaulting over the horse to the ground on the other side without touching the saddle, is remarkably nervy and hard to do."

On the following day Ty again was complimented as he and Ambrose Stahl did difficult roping and riding stunts.

W. J. Cole had a bad day on the famous bull called Ringtail. Astride Ringtail, Cole lasted only three "bucks."

Today a favorite event in the rodeo is called the Bareback Stampede. The 1965 program describes it: "At a given signal all sixteen of the arena chute gates open and sixteen bareback riders explode into the arena in a pile-driving, sunfishing, perilous stampede for the finish line."

The 1916 version was called The Thrilling Wild Horse Race. A rider who was particularly responsible for the "thrills" was Frank Greenway, a Negro cowboy. The event and Frank's part in it were described in the newspaper:

"Its concentrated action, spliced by the quick moves of the never-before-ridden wild horses—horses with the spirit of freedom as their heritage—makes this race exciting as well as uncertain in its outcome. When the starting pistol sounds, the riders are off; some of them around the track and some off the ground. This race is not won by getting a good lead, as the leading horse may stop dead still 20 feet from the finish and refuse to move farther. Half the excitement of the race is in watching the numerous vaqueros hold and saddle the wild ones. If anyone thinks these creatures ever felt a rider's weight, let him watch their frantic fights against being held and saddled. Some buck and run, others lie down, and one stands up on his hind feet and strikes with the fore feet viciously. The wild roan didn't get into the first race nor the race of the second day. Both days he broke and ran away around the track pursued by half a dozen cowboys. By the time he was caught and saddled the race was over.

"Frank Greenway, No. 8, the fearless Negro cowboy, likes to help saddle the fiercest of the herd. In helping saddle a bay pony he went down with the horse when it fell and found himself between the four kicking feet of the prone animal. Greenway saved his bacon by taking a dive across the pony's body, sliding head first to the ground behind the creature's back."

Ty Stokes and Frank Greenway were both crowd pleasers, but the real star of the rodeo for many years was the Negro cowboy Jesse Stahl. He first appeared in the 1913 rodeo, when he entered the bulldogging contest. His performance apparently pleased the crowd, for the newspaper reported that he received both laughter and cheers.

In the next year's rodeo, Jesse Stahl entered the bronc riding contest. His entry was unlucky. He drew a horse named One-Eyed Riley and was promptly "piled" on the floor of the arena. He did better in other events, however. He rode a previously unconquered mule, and he mastered the locally famous bucking bull named Ringtail.

When he returned to the rodeo in 1916, he was a favorite of the crowd and a star performer. A newspaperman wrote that Jesse "caused the most excitement of all by riding backwards an unsaddled, blindfolded wild horse. The bucking bronc ran into the corral fence, which scared him so badly he ran away with Stahl."

But that was not all. "The popular Negro rider appeared again, riding the vicious steed whose cognomen is 'Glasseye.' Stahl won, but he had to work for the plaudits of the crowd. After the match Stahl was escorted across the field to a position near the grandstand; the crowd cheered him, while the Cowboy band stood up and played."

According to the newspaper accounts, the California Rodeos held in Salinas were as exciting as any rodeos put on anywhere. Year after year the Negro cowboys made significant contributions to their success.

Jesse's biggest success may have come on July 21, 1917. The newspaper account said that "The feature of Saturday afternoon's concluding events was the case of Jesse Stahl vs. Coyote. The *peerless* Negro rode the hitherto unridden Coyote. This feat was nothing short of marvelous. Many a man has tried to ride the famous sorrel bucker, the hitherto champion of all bucking broncos, but without success. Four and one-fifth seconds was the longest time anyone had ever remained on Coyote. Coyote whirled round and round. His revolutions were made with great speed. Stahl rode him twenty seconds. Then the cowboys stopped the contest. Stahl's feat was an enviable one."

Year after year Jesse won the "bulldogging" contest, the "bull riding" contest, and the "bucking" contest. At the rodeo in the summer of 1920 Jesse successfully rode the "famous outlaw mare, Shimmie Sue." A newspaper reporter then wrote that Jesse Stahl was the best wildhorse rider in the West.

✺ʒɑ CHAPTER **17**

The End of the Trails

✺ʒɑ The trail driving days lasted little more than twenty-five years after the Civil War. During that time Texas cattlemen and cowboys helped to settle and stock the empty lands of Kansas, Nebraska, Colorado, Wyoming, South Dakota, and Montana. There they found open country, hundreds of millions of acres of empty rangeland. In Wyoming alone they spread their cattle over nearly fifty million acres of unfenced land.

Yet these vast spaces could be crowded. As more and more cattlemen started ranches, even the rich grasslands of Wyoming and Montana began to fill up with more cattle than they could support. Cattlemen began to string hundreds of miles of barbed wire fences to protect their pastures, and these fences helped to slow down the great cattle drives.

The whole cattle business suffered a great shock in 1886. It began in the summer, which was one of the hottest and dustiest on record. All through Dakota, Montana, and

Wyoming cattle suffered as water holes dried up and grass turned brown. By the end of July, many streams had run low or stopped. Fires started up and roared through the dry grass of the plains. By the end of summer the best of the winter pastures had been destroyed.

Then came the worst winter ever to strike the northern ranges. Temperatures dropped to zero in November and even lower in December. By January, when sixteen inches of snow fell in a few days and Montana temperatures went down to forty-five degrees below zero, some animals froze to death standing. Herds drifted helplessly, weakened by lack of food or water. They pawed at the snow, trying to get through an icy crust that cut their legs and noses. Thousans of cattle died.

One Montana historian, describing the misfortunes of the cattlemen, said, "the most fortunate lost half of their stock, but many of the losses exceeded 75 per cent." The catastrophe was dramatized by Charles Russell, a cowboy artist working in Montana. When his boss wrote in the spring of 1887 to ask about his cattle, Russell made a famous answer. On a postcard he drew a poor starved cow standing on shaky legs. Underneath the picture he wrote, "The Last of 5000."

Throughout all of the West the cattlemen suffered. The big blizzards of 1886–1887 demonstrated the dangers of the open range. At the same time thousands of homesteaders were coming West and settling in the valleys and along the streams. When they fenced their farms, they shut off access to water. Most of the cattlemen began to realize that the old days of big herds, long drives, and great roundups were over. They withdrew to lands that they owned or leased. They began growing hay, and they reduced the size of their herds as they improved the quality of their stock.

Even in New Mexico, where the climate was kinder than in Montana, cattlemen now favored smaller ranches. Writing in 1890, the governor of New Mexico reported: "After years of experience, the owners of cattle have demonstrated that the business of cattle-ranging on the open ranges is not profitable. There is a disposition to smaller holdings and to confine the cattle in inclosed pastures. Prominent ranchmen express the opinion that 500 cows confined in pastures will produce more profit than 5,000 on the open ranges."

Not all cattlemen agreed. Some of them wanted to hold the open range, even though they did not own it. They resented the arrival of homesteaders, and in some parts of the old West the big men tried to drive out the little men.

In Wyoming the strong feeling between these two groups burst into flame with the famous Johnson County War. A group of wealthy cattlemen decided to strike against the homesteaders. They claimed the farmers were "rustling" cattle. So the cattlemen made up a small army of toughs and hired gunmen and moved against the "rustlers" of Johnson County.

They struck first at the small KC Ranch, killing two men. Then they moved on toward Buffalo, the county seat. But they soon learned that the homesteaders could also organize. Sheriff Angus of Buffalo moved with a much larger force against the cattlemen. The cattlemen and their gunmen retreated to the deserted TA Ranch, where they barricaded themselves and prepared to withstand a siege.

Now the cattlemen's situation became desperate. Instead

of being man hunters, they were the hunted. They were surrounded by a large and angry force of armed men. They raised rough fortifications, and they had enough water. But they were trapped. As hours and days wore on, their situation grew nearly hopeless.

News of their desperate plight finally reached Cheyenne. There Acting Governor Barber learned that some of the "best citizens" of Wyoming were in great danger. Governor Barber wired President Harrison that a revolt was in progress and asked him for Federal troops.

Meanwhile the situation of the cattlemen and their hired gunmen had become worse. Sheriff Angus and his men remodeled a hay wagon into a fortified movable platform. They loaded the wagon—they called it a "go-devil"—with dynamite and prepared to push it against the ranch house where the cattlemen and their gunmen were trapped. If the sheriff had been able to carry out his plan, all the men in the ranch would have been doomed. Nothing could have kept them from being blasted, burned, shot, or hanged.

But the United States cavalry—three companies of Negro troopers—rode on the scene just in time. The cattlemen and their gunmen surrendered to the Federal troops, who took them into custody. So they were saved from the vengeance of the settlers they had sought to kill or terrify. The settlers could only watch as the cavalry led the cattlemen away.

Among the watchers was Floyd Bard, then a boy of fourteen. "I got to see all of them," he said, "as they were being marched from the TA Ranch to Fort McKinney, two miles south of Buffalo. All told there were fifty of them. They rode horseback in pairs, with a Negro soldier riding on either side. First in this parade were the cowmen. Then came about ten of their seasoned killers. Bringing up the rear were the hired Texans. They were a sorry-looking lot with their stubble beards, and eyes that looked like burned holes in a blanket. They had not shaved for a week, had had very little sleep and nothing much to eat while bottled up in the TA ranch house."

With the end of the Johnson County War, even the cattlemen in Wyoming began to realize that the old days of the open range were over. Like the ranchers in other states, they bought the land they needed, and they reduced the size of their ranches. Consequently the number of cowboys they employed was also reduced.

Most of the Negro cowboys who had ridden up the trails with longhorn cattle eventually returned to Texas. But some of them stayed on in all the states of the North.

In Wyoming for instance, one Negro cowboy who stayed was Jim Simpson. With another Negro cowboy, Joe Proctor, Jim went to work for the Flying E Ranch. Jim was a good hand who became known as "about the best roper on the range." When he grew older and heavier he turned to driving a chuck wagon and cooking.

As a ranch and roundup cook he earned a fine reputation. He also became a friend and adviser to the younger cowboys who did not know much about range life. He tried to protect them against dangerous mistakes, and he nursed them when they were hurt or sick.

On roundups, Jim was a respected member of the crew, whether he hired on as a cowboy or, in later years, as a cook. When the weather was bad, the crew all slept in a big tent, and when the weather was good, they slept outside. When Jim was a cook, everybody helped to drag in his wood. When he yelled, "Come and get her," the crew took care to keep from raising dust or messing up his camp.

Although Jim knew his trade, building good cooking fires, keeping his pots and pans clean, and serving the best possible food, he had the problems that come with the rough conditions on the high Wyoming ranges.

One night, for example, a heavy snow fell. In the morning everyone was cold. The cowboys ran foot races to keep warm while Jim worked on his fire. As fast as he built it, the wind blew it out. That morning it was ten o'clock before the cowboys had breakfast.

During the winter, Jim played his fiddle for "kitchen dances." They were called this because often the kitchen of a small ranch house was the only room available for dancing. Only four couples were allowed on the floor in a square dance. "Most always there were four times as many men as there were women. The men didn't get enough dancing even with daylight just around the corner. With the women folks it was different. They were ready to drop in their tracks, but they wouldn't own up to it. Jim Simpson, the roundup cook, was usually the fiddler, and a good one."

During the winter, too, Jim was welcomed at the homes and ranches of his many friends. He spent at least two winters at the George Harper ranch. He assisted Mrs. Harper, who had lost a hand from blood poisoning but still had to care for her four small children. Jim took over.

A few years later Jim Simpson was caught in a situation like a scene in an old Western movie in which shy cowboys kiss only their horses. Although women and children were becoming more important in Wyoming society, the Flying

E Ranch remained "a bachelor stronghold." As a result, when a newly married schoolteacher arrived at the ranch, all its cowboys scattered.

The story was printed in *Annals of Wyoming:* "when the new bride stopped one day to get warm while on the way to Buffalo, the assembled cowboys gave one glance and disappeared like magic, leaving Jim Simpson, a Negro round-up cook, fiddler and expert roper, to entertain her."

Another cowboy who stayed in Wyoming was Bronco Sam, the same one who had ridden a steer through the plate glass window in Cheyenne. He worked for many years on a ranch near Laramie, and he became locally famous for his skill and courage. Even today there are a few old-timers who like to spin yarns about Bronco Sam's actions and abilities.

Other Negroes stayed in the cattle business, but that business began to change rapidly. By the beginning of this century, many of the old cowboys had left the range to take other jobs. Some became rodeo performers. Others became farmers. Deadwood Dick became a Pullman porter.

Even in Texas where land is most plentiful, many large operations were abandoned. The story of the big XIT ranch shows how the cattle business changed.

In 1886 the XIT ranch owned 3,000,000 acres of land in ten counties of the Texas Panhandle. It grew until it had as many as 150,000 head of cattle, and its cowboys rode along 6,000 miles of barbed wire fence.

This incredibly large ranch, which sprawled over an area greater than some Eastern states, hired both white and Negro cowboys. Together they fought prairie fires and storms, broke horses, strung fence, and drove cattle. Some of the

Negroes were Jo Johnson, a cowboy named Hal, and one named Big Joe.

One old-timer remembered bunkhouse "shindigs" during which some of the Negroes danced while other cowboys watched and applauded. "Their particular favorite," he said, "was Big Joe, whose real fame came neither from his cowpunching nor his sideline of banjo-picking, but from a pair of the most enormous feet any of the other cowhands had ever laid eyes on. Big Joe's feet got that way from going barefoot all summer. He even rode barefoot!"

At least two of the XIT's cooks were Negroes. One of them was Jim Perry, remembered by many men as the best cook they had ever known. Both were top hands and good riders. One white cowboy frequently tried to ride mean, unbroken horses, but he admitted that Jim Perry was better at it. "If they throwed me," he said, "Jim would ride them for me."

At one time the XIT ranch employed more than 150 men to ride its millions of acres. But then the cattle business began to change, and its enormous size ceased to be profitable. It began to sell off its land and cattle. By the time of the first World War, the XIT had fired all its cowboys and sold all its herds. Thereafter it sold its land.

Only a few giant ranches are left today. Of these, perhaps the King Ranch is the largest and the best known.

Today a visitor to the King Ranch can spend a week and never see a cowboy. The foreman drives a Buick sedan, and most of his crew drive or ride in trucks. Many of the men are specialists—tractor men, windmill men, drivers of heavy earth-moving equipment. Much of their talk is about machinery, government regulations, or veterinary medicine.

The ranch does have eighty men who sometimes ride horses, but their work is far different from that of the old cowboys who rode the original cattle trails. If the foreman is asked how many cowboys he has, he replies, "Well, we don't use the word cowboy."

But there are still some Negro cowboys riding on southern ranges. Some herd cattle in Florida. Others work on Texas ranches, particularly along the Gulf Coast. On some ranches all the hands are Negroes. And there are a few Negro cowboys working in all the cattle country of the West, on both northern and southern ranges.

One Negro cowboy was still herding cattle long after automobiles and tractors had begun to change the old West. He is remembered today because he followed some cattle up a canyon and made a great scientific discovery.

He was George McJunkin, who in his youth rode on several drives out of Texas and worked in the 1920's on the old Shoemaker ranch near Folsom, New Mexico. A good bronc buster and a top hand, he was also a collector of Indian arrowheads.

One spring day McJunkin followed the trail of some straying cattle up an arroyo known as Dead Horse Gulch. Glancing across the gulch at the other side, he noticed some bones sticking out of the bank. They looked a little like cow bones, but they were buried many feet below the surface. The strange sight made him curious; so he got off his horse, and slid down the side of the gulch and began to investigate. Prying with his knife, he soon loosened a chipped flint point different from any arrowhead he had ever seen. He took it with him, and eventually carried both his story and his unusual flint point to a scientist.

The scientist was interested in the bones in which the cowboy had found the flint, and the bones were identified as those of an Ice Age bison, an animal that lived 10,000 years ago.

George McJunkin, a modern Negro cowboy and bronc buster, had discovered some remains left by an Ice Age hunting party. By doing so he had rolled back the history of early America a hundred centuries.

Index

139